W9-CEB-881

Battered Women in Korean Immigrant Families

GARLAND LIBRARY OF SOCIOLOGY
VOLUME 29
GARLAND REFERENCE LIBRARY OF SOCIAL SCIENCE
VOLUME 903

Garland Library of Sociology

Peter W. Cookson, Jr., *Series Editor*

Battered Women in Korean Immigrant Families

The Silent Scream

Young I. Song

Garland Publishing, Inc.
New York and London
1996

Library of Congress Cataloging-in-Publication Data

Song, Young I. (Young In)
Battered women in Korean immigrant families : the silent scream / by Young I. Song.
p. cm. — (Garland library of sociology ; vol. 29) (Garland reference library of social science ; vol. 903)
Includes bibliographical references.
ISBN 0-8153-1320-9
1. Korean American women—Abuse of. 2. Wife abuse—United States. I. Title. II. Series. III. Series: Garland reference library of social science ; v. 903.
HV6626.2.S66 1996
362.82'92'089957073—dc20 93–33899
CIP

Printed on acid-free, 250-year-life paper
Manufactured in the United States of America

To Kristine, Jennifer and Michelle

Series Editor's Preface

Perhaps we will never know the extent to which women are victimized throughout the world. Conceptualizing victimization as a continuum of abuse, it is probably safe to say that very few women escape male aggression. Sexual abuse of women can be apparently subtle or extremely blatant; the abuse of women is manifested in the public arena and in private relationships. Abuse can be directed against strangers, colleagues, and even alleged loved ones. Much of the violence against women is not reported; it is believed that only one in ten rapes are reported to public authorities. Without fear of exaggeration, we may say that sexual abuse is so common that it has become part of the very fabric of society.

This sense that sexual abuse is part of the taken-for-granted social reality demands that men and women bear witness to the causes and consequences of behavior that is deeply anti-social and destructive. Young I. Song's *Battered Women in Korean Immigrant Families: The Silent Scream* reveals the fate of women who have little or no public voice—hence the subtitle, *The Silent Scream*. Professor Song has written a powerful book about a little known group. Her book examines the cultural origins of why Korean women have tolerated dehumanization. She places this situation in the context of cultural conflict as it affects immigrant families and contextualizes her study in theories of domestic violence. Her study is original and her findings are an important contribution to the understanding of cultural conflict and wife abuse. Her work illuminates how "battering" is a physical expression of a male ideology based on the belief that women should be subservient to men. When this belief becomes a cultural norm, systematic dehumanization becomes possible—even "acceptable." In a general sense, this process by which ideology justifies symbolic and physical violence is the origin of a great deal of human suffering. Who speaks for the sufferers, especially those who have no public voice? Fortunately, Professor Song has the courage and training to give voice to those who suffer in silence.

The Garland Library of Sociology, therefore, is privileged to include *Battered Women in Korean Immigrant Families* in its series of first-rate sociological studies. Now, more than ever, there is a need to publish sociological research that addresses the critical issues of our era. It is our aim that the studies published in this series will be read by readers who are deeply concerned about the present condition of society and the future direction of our culture. The role of the Garland Library of Sociology is to bring to the public those books that will advance our understanding of society and encourage us to engage in the resolution of those contradictions and injustices that keep our society from reaching its potential.

I hope that this book will be read by individuals who have a commitment to scholarship and to societal reform. This study is especially recommended for those interested in gender, immigrations, and culture. This book has the capacity to open our minds and to inform us about the complex and difficult world in which we live.

Peter W. Cookson, Jr.

ACKNOWLEDGEMENT

I am grateful to many people who have contributed in countless ways to the development of this book. I would especially like to express my heartfelt appreciation to the 150 Korean women, although I cannot individually thank each one, who volunteered to open their lives to me despite their pain. Gratitude is expressed to Esther Choi and Nellie Byun who provided dedicated efforts in preparing manuscripts.

Special acknowledgement goes to Dr. Daniel Lee at Loyola University, Chicago, whose dedication to social work and minorities in America has indeed been an inspiration to me. My gratitude is also extended to my mother for her love and prayers which helped to keep me along the way. Finally, thanks goes to my daughter Kristine. Without Kristine's assistance and deep understanding, this book could not have been completed.

CONTENTS

INTRODUCTION

"Forgive me, forgive me!" the young woman begged her husband. The woman was so frightened she burst into soundless tears. This was the scene as she rushed into my house, barefoot and clad only in her undergarments, saying barely audibly in a trembling voice to my mother, "Hide me in a safe place, please!" The abused woman was followed by her knife-wielding husband. I was only seven years old when I was awakened by her crying in the middle of the night.

That night, I could not fall back to sleep right away after I recognized her as a lady who lived in the corner of my village. I wondered what she could possibly have done that was so bad as to make her beg for forgiveness. It puzzled me, since she was always a polite, cheerful, and kind woman who was favored by all the village children. That remained a big question in my mind. Perhaps that was one of the incentives that moved me to do research on battered Korean women. In fact, on numerous occasions while I was conducting this study, I wanted to stand up and announce to those hurt women that they had no right to be hurt. My objective in writing this book is to convince people who find themselves in similar situations to realize the tremendous pain of the hurting relationships and to provide options to ease the pain and ameliorate the situation.

The most important motivating factor in writing this book was the keen personal interest I have always felt in the lives of contemporary Korean women, especially those who hold their traditional views in one hand and western views in the other. I come by this interest quite naturally, having grown up in the crossfire of cultural conflict between career-minded, independent modern Korean women and the conservatism inherited from the predominantly Confucian tradition which still binds them. Historically, wife abuse has been tolerated in traditional Korean culture, and I wondered if these Korean women, especially those who live in the urban cities in the United States, experience wife abuse in the midst of cultural adjustment. It occurred to me that a study of their experiences might reveal insights into the nature of the wife abuse they experienced in cultural adjustment and, further, reveal the consequences and ways of managing these abuses.

Korean communities in the United States are rapidly growing. Undoubtedly, Korean women play important roles in the life of Korean immigrants through which women have influenced the Korean community. I wanted to learn what kinds of women aspire to the nonbattered relationship, how it is acquired, maintained, and what impact it has on the abused women themselves, their families, the Korean immigrant society, and more indirectly, on the Asian American society. Still another consideration were the current myths about "quiet" Asian Americans, including Korean immigrants, which tend to hide wife abuse in Korean immigrant families. Furthermore, as the following folk tale illustrates, being a Korean woman means that she has no voice, no other role options but to silently tolerate marital hardships, including abuse.

Once upon a time a man said to his daughter when she was setting out to go to her wedding, "A woman's life is very hard. She must pretend that she does not see the things that are to be seen, that she does not hear the words spoken around her, and she must speak as little as possible." So for three years after her marriage, the woman never spoke a word.

Thus, a virtuous Korean woman should remain dumb three years, deaf another three years, and blind still another three years in order to weather the hardships, tribulations, and abuse in married life. This further supports the passivism of being unnecessarily quiet.

Perhaps you wonder why I am writing about this old tradition. Does this have anything to do with Korean immigrant women? Harvey (1980) stated that Koreans are inclined to feel that neither their national character nor their individual behavior can be fully understood without historical reference. Their almost obsessive preoccupation with history is particularly pronounced with reference to Confucianism.

Osgood (1951) wrote: " ... however much modern Korean people may seem encrusted with other beliefs, hidden Confucian values will show up beneath a scratch." Other observers of Koreans generally concur with him (Brandt, 1971; Crane, 1967, 1972; and Rutt, 1967). Despite revolutionary changes which have marked almost every aspect of their lives, especially in the present century among immigrants' lives in the United States, the Koreans feel an abiding and deep sense of identity with their cultural past and conscious efforts to perpetuate it. Such cultural persistence is especially strong in the institution of marriage and the phenomenon of wife abuse.

What peculiarly signalizes the situation of woman is that she -- a free and autonomous being like all human creatures -- nevertheless finds herself living in a world where men compel her to assume the status of the other.

Simone de Beauvoir

CHAPTER 1

What Led to This Point

The history of wife abuse can be traced from the early Middle Ages (Gies and Gies, 1978). It is only recently that society has begun to seriously challenge the long-standing tradition which allows a man to batter his spouse. In order to fully understand the nature of domestic violence, it is necessary to consider wife beating with regard to both the socio-cultural context in which it presently occurs and its historical precedent (Hofeller, 1982).

In all societies, women have been and continue to be the victims of physical and psychological abuse. Throughout history, men have been the decision-makers and the lawmakers. Women have been treated as second-class citizens. Violence against women finds its basis in women's minority status and their historically subordinate position in society.

A minority group is one that is socially, politically, and economically subordinate; its members are excluded from various opportunities which limit their freedom of choice and self-development. They tend to have lower self-esteem and often become the objects of contempt, ridicule, and violence; generally, they are socially isolated (Feldman, 1983).

In terms of this definition, Korean immigrant women are a minority group within another minority group in the United States. Korean culture can be considered an outstanding example of the patriarchal society which has been in existence for many centuries. The large patriarchal family was the basic organizational unit in Korea, and a woman's position was subservient to man where inequality was more formal than real.

According to Kate Millett, patriarchal societies have had a history of suppression, which graded the relationship between men and women to that of rule and obedience, thus oppressing the women through culture and system. Patriarchal societies have also had a history of savagery and cruelty in regard to women. These societies have promoted the fraudulent beliefs that a woman is weak, wicked, inferior, etc. through myth, religion, and scholarship (Millett, 1971).

Wife beating is an expression of patriarchal domination, the origin of which lies in the subordination of females and in their subjection to male authority and control. This relationship between women and men has been institutionalized in the structure of the patriarchal family and is supported by the economic and political institutions and by the culture's belief system (Dobash and Dobash, 1979).

Korean women have had a long history of oppression, exploitation, and enslavement. These victims of battering, who have not even had the right to express their humanity, have been exploited and dehumanized for generations. Battered women have learned to adjust to Korean life by taking it as the "destiny" or "fate" which their very entry into this world as women imposed upon them. Since no alternative was imaginable, they were compelled to make the tremendously difficult adjustment to this lifestyle by making virtue out of necessity. Thus the women of Korea, who have endured a life of subjugation to men longer and to a harsher extent than most others in the world, are among the slowest and most reluctant to recognize and admit the injustice of their situation. Women's liberation is a concept still very much taboo in Korea. No one who wants to be part of "respectable" society dares to be identified as a women's rights advocate (Lee, 1977).

The battering of women, like other crimes of violence against women, has been justified in the context of Korean culture. A traditional Korean saying that "the real taste of dried fish and women can only be derived from beating them once every three days" has been often quoted as a rationale for "beating" women, thus justifying the violent act as a means of improving their behavior. It perpetuates the notion that a man should beat a woman when she does something that makes him angry. In other words, the oppressed Korean woman's acknowledgment of her oppression would be a negation of her only source of pride, namely, to serve man as a "wise" mother and "good wife." A Korean woman who is repeatedly abused by her husband accepts this and considers it her personal shame and misfortune. She fails to see any relationship between these actions and the question of equality between the sexes.

Lee (1977) believes that Korean women developed an ability to absorb insults and injuries without protest and to assume responsibilities for others' faults; in contrast, Korean men were incapable of bearing responsibility for their own actions, always seeking to blame others. Since this is also reflected in the societal attitudes, it is important to remember the existence of the victim's precipitation ideology, and thus blame the abuse on it.

The lives of Korean immigrant women in the United States are an extension of thousands of years of battering, which is compounded by the problems and frustration caused by cultural conflict. Although these immigrant families came to the United States to better their lives, not many were ready to confront life in the United States, particularly with regard to the cultural differences. Regardless of each Korean's motivation for immigration to the United States, there are drastic differences between the lives of Korean and American families, differences which often cause misunderstanding and frustrations when the two cultures come into contact with one another. Korean immigrant society at the present time is undergoing a stage of transition in which Korean traditional social structures and norms are breaking down and have not yet been replaced by clearly discernible Western norms. Thus, Korean immigrant couples are subjected to various factors that determine how they are to behave and feel both before and after transplantation into a new culture. Subsequently, battering women is influenced either negatively by cultural conflict or positively during the process of cultural adjustment. As a consequence, the problem of wife abuse among Korean immigrants must be viewed in terms of the cultural context.

While all of these beliefs have perpetuated the mistaken notion among Korean women that the victim has precipitated her own abuse, the present study attempts to broaden the perspective of conjugal violence by examining the subcultural normative system with cultural tolerance. The Korean women's cultural background and their attitude of traditional role rigidity, coupled with stress-evoking environments such as the language barrier and underemployment, tend to create a phenomenon that is reflected in the behavior and psychological traits of the Korean battered families in the United States.

Although concern over the occurrence of wife abuse is not a new phenomenon, the study of it is a relatively recent aspect of scholarly inquiry. The need for more empirical data on wife abuse has been addressed elsewhere (Davidson, 1977; Gelles, 1972; Langley and Levy, 1978; Walker, 1979; Hofeller, 1982). In the case of Korean women, there has been no comprehensive study conducted to date. Korean battered women, a minority within an ethnic and sexual minority, have received almost no attention in the social research literature, nor have they received the social services provided for minority women.

Until ten years ago, the number of Korean immigrants in the United States was negligible, and their problems were less obvious. Thus the difficulties they encountered were ignored. At the present time, however, the situation has changed. In 1965 only one out of every fourteen immigrants to the United States was Asian; by 1973, the figure had risen to approximately one out of every three new immigrants admitted to America (Sanders,

1978). Korean immigrants are one of the largest groups entering the United States, and their rate of increase has been higher than any other immigrant group from Asia. People from India, Korea and the Philippines account for about 50% of the total number of Asian immigrants (Kim and Brown, 1985).

A majority of recent Korean immigrant families has come to the United States, not so much for survival itself, but rather to elevate or to improve their opportunities. In contrast to their motives for immigration, however, many Korean immigrant families in the United States, upon arrival, experience a great deal of difficulty. Each member of the Korean immigrant family faces serious problems. Moreover, the women seem to encounter more hardships than any of the other family members. Data from materials drawn from the case files of the Korean-American Mental Health Center in Los Angeles suggest that there has been a noticeable increase in marital conflict and conjugal violence in the Korean community of Los Angeles (Yim, 1978). Abuse of women constitutes a high proportion of the center's caseload. It has also been noted that almost two-thirds of those cases involve extreme violence. The problems related to wife abuse that are frequently encountered in clinical treatments include severe depression, child abuse, various symptoms of somatization, physical injuries, and a high incidence of suicide attempts (Song, 1982).

The complete lack of research on the Korean battered woman does not indicate that they do not have any serious problems, but rather, it suggests that existing problems have not yet been thoroughly examined and documented. As Ryu (1977) indicated, demographic studies of the Korean-Americans have been severely limited in the United States by the unavailability of baseline data and by the limited nature of existing data. As the population of Korean women in America increases and becomes more visible, family problems and service needs also increase. During the period of cultural adjustment, Korean immigrant women experience a heightened sense of vulnerability as they suffer from both the deep-rooted, traditional cultural biases against women and the strains caused by the cultural barriers as well as their unfamiliarity with the use of social resources.

Unfortunately, battering incidents do occur in these contexts. Problems experienced by Korean women might have been overlooked in the past either because of their relatively small numbers or of the assumption that Asian-Americans "take care of their own" and "rarely become social problems" (Kalish and Yuen, 1971). Abuse of women is not an unknown or a surprising issue to the Korean immigrants in the United States. Since the battering of women has been traditionally viewed as not a social problem in Korea, it continues to be similarly viewed by Korean immigrants. It has always been seen as a matter which is to be dealt with by the family members.

Battered women among Korean immigrants are silent victims who have been continuously hidden by closed boundaries such as culture and custom. Unlike other recent Asian immigrant women from Hong Kong, the Philippines and India, Korean immigrant women are severely handicapped by their unfamiliarity with Western culture, particularly with the use of the English language, largely because Korea has never had an Anglo-Saxon colonial experience (Lee, D.B., 1980). The problems faced by these women are further complicated by the fact that many Korean battered women are ignorant of available services or are reluctant to seek help due to cultural conflict; these problems go untreated and remain liabilities to the community as a whole. Consequently, these Korean immigrant battered women will continue to be isolated, and their problems with battering will increase.

If you let a woman pass three days
without any beating, she
will turn into a fox.

Korean Proverb

CHAPTER 2

How/Why Korean Women Have Tolerated Dehumanization

Did They Have a Choice?

Korean immigrant women are confronted with Western culture and new lives in a Western country, and to a great degree, they have retained Korean traditions that cannot be disregarded. Focusing on Korean womanhood from traditional to current aspects will help to provide insightful understanding of immigrant women from Korea.

Korea is a country of morals, ethics, and conventions. Confucianism played a leading role, greatly influencing the degradation of women's status in Korean society. The function of the woman within the teaching of Korean traditional thought was simple and clear: to "obey your father before your marriage, then your husband after the marriage, and after your husband dies, obey your son" (Mace and Mace, 1959). Thus, a Korean woman's life cycle was divided into three major stages in terms of the men she had to obey at each stage.

Throughout Korean history, a woman's obedience was unquestionable and absolute. In Korean society, a virtuous traditional Korean woman is without talent or intellectual achievement. Korean women have been the most afflicted single majority group in the country. In spite of superficial improvements in recent years, Korean women's social roles and status have changed very little. Therefore, the most powerful and original force in the dehumanization process today may be referred to as that of injustice based on sex in Korea (Kim, D. S., 1978).

The relation between man and woman can be considered to be the first unfair human relation that produced self-worship, power-abuse, and has been the psychological basis of all other suppression and rule (Mill, 1970). Firestone (1970) contends that today's modern civilization was established on the sacrifice of woman's sensuality-culture. Dehumanization of women brings on dehumanization of men, and therefore, misery for the entire society. Although the number of educated women has gradually increased lately, Korean women are still under severe social restrictions. They are still being discriminated against in various spheres of society and are victims of oppression. As Beauvoir indicated, the status of the woman has been improved, but not basically changed (Beauvoir, 1957).

One example of the Korean women's position is concubinage. Though it is now officially defunct, a functioning family system of concubinage, where a man could practice polygamy to perpetuate his family lineage if his wife could not produce sons (Son, 1978), still exists. Yet, concubinage was prevalent among those who did have sons. The practice of concubinage made a woman simply a sex object, besides making her a constant threat to the wife. Thus, the idea of male dominance still prevails. According to the Research Institute of Behavior Science in Seoul, 50% of all Korean women in maternity wards said in a survey that if they could not bear a son, they would even try to get a son through a second wife of their husband (Son, 1978). Son further describes two psychological reasons for this kind of answer: (1) a mother does not want to have a daughter to whom the heritage of suffering and insult will be transferred; (2) a mother deserves human treatment only when she bears a son.

Until she gave birth to a son, a wife felt as if she "sat on a cushion of needles." With the birth of a son, her duty was fulfilled in perpetuating the ancestral lineage, and she found protection and security in the future of her son. Even treatment during the postpartum period exemplified the difference of the sexes. After giving birth to a son, the young mother was encouraged to lie quietly in bed for two or three weeks. However, if the mother bore a girl and lay in bed more than one week, she was put to shame or had to suffer an insult. In Kyongsang Province, noted as the stronghold of Confucianism, it was customary for the mother-in-law to prepare a feast for the birth of a grandson. If, however, a girl child was born, the mother-in-law immediately left the house and would not return for almost a week as an expression of regret and disappointment for the birth of a baby girl. This disappointment was even transmitted to the female infants by the way they were named-- "Soun" (disappointment), "Sop-Sop" (pity), or "Ukam" (regret) (Rhim, 1978; Moose, 1911).

Even in the best of circumstances, being born female constituted a liability not only to the self but to those, in particular the mother, on whom the infant was dependent for nurture and protection. This is not to say that daughters were regularly mistreated, nor that they were not sometimes indulged by parents and grandparents. Rather, the point is that even when parents and grandparents found delight in a female baby, their enjoyment of her was quiet and private. If they spoiled a girl baby, they did so almost surreptitiously. And for those with insufficient resources to support another life or without a son, the birth of a daughter posed an excessive economic burden. Some parents sought relief from such predicaments by selling their daughters as permanently indentured servants (or slaves before the prohibition of slavery), as apprentices for the *kisaeng* (a singing and dancing girl) role, or as potential wives.

Another form of mistreatment of women can be traced in the separation of the sexes. When boys and girls reached the age of seven, they were not allowed to sit together. Korean women were strictly segregated from the men in the family. Even the architecture of the house, whatever its scale, separated it into male and female spheres. Generally, the male quarters faced outward toward the external world, while the female quarters were protected behind it and separated from it by a courtyard. Access to the male quarters was strictly governed. Division of labor by sex was such that it made them indispensably and mutually dependent, though segregated in actual activities.

On the street or in public it was the rule for the wife to walk several steps behind the husband. When a woman walked down the street, she wore a long cloak over a white special jacket, called *jang-ot,* which covered her face, leaving only two eyes peeping out, to hide her face from the sight of men (*The Dong-A-Ilbo*, 1975).

However, due to influences of the Western culture, the shadow of the old-style women in *jang-ot* has disappeared, and yet their attitude toward men is still little changed. To address men familiarly is disdained and condemned as the manners of *kisaeng*. Any modest Korean woman usually assumes a blunt air and pays no compliments even to her husband in the presence of other people. Women were inevitably cut off from opportunities for independence in social activities. Even now in Korean society, high school girls are not allowed to associate with male friends by school rules. Even some Christian Korean churches have separate seating for men and women. In the event of marriage, there are restrictions which are quite noticeable. In the West, one falls in love, then marries. In Korea, one marries, then falls in love. Korean young people must have patience to wait for the marriage arrangement or face the hatred of their parents, relatives and neighbors. Thus, marriage in Korea does not involve the personal choice of the couple, but instead it involves the consideration of ancestors, descendents, property, and educational compatibility (Moon, 1978). In traditional Korean society, Korean women had nothing to say about their marriage, and above all, they never saw their husbands until the wedding night. Marriage created a totally different status in a woman's life compared to a man's life as a husband.

The marriage arrangement was generally achieved by first making marriage a matter of negotiation between two households with little or no personal participation by the prospective mates. Women were made utterly dependent on socially recognized relationships to men for their own duties and identities. Their existence was defined by reference to men and justified by their usefulness to them. Women were, for all their indispensability to the society, ancillary people and were readily replaceable as individuals.

Even when a woman married, her continued right to remain in the husband's household was contingent upon others' evaluation of her performance. Thus women were not only socially tangential to men, but they also continually had to validate their duties in order to retain them. For example, women could not under any circumstance initiate divorce, but a woman could be divorced on any one of the seven legitimate standards and rules for marriage. If the woman broke any one of the rules, she was unconditionally divorced. These were: (1) to serve her parents-in-law well; (2) to produce children, particularly males; (3) to not be lecherous; (4) to not be too jealous; (5) to not have an incurable disease; (6) to not talk too much; or (7) to not steal (Lee, 1967). Under these circumstances, women had no legitimate economic autonomy (Choi, 1966). Also, and most important, women considered acceptance and adherence to these conditions of their sex role as the highest virtue.

In other words, divorce was a one-sided expulsion, a fate regarded as worse than death by women of respectable families. The parents of the women thus expelled refused to receive them back because they believed it was a great dishonor. At best, her parents could exert only the most indirect influence on her personal welfare. Since a married woman had no legitimate role in her natal household, if she failed in marriage it usually meant that she was permanently deprived of the only legitimate role through which she could participate in the society. From this point of view, Korean women did not have any alternative but to endure and suffer.

Traditional Socialization of Korean Women's Lives

In terms of life cycle, Korean women lived through three major stages: premarital life in the natal household; postmarital, patrilocal life; and retirement. Each stage was subdivided into a more or less distinct period marked by a transition in the socialization of the women. The premarital stage consisted of infancy, childhood, and post-pubescence. The postmarital stage began with a period of mutual assessment and adjustment, progressing through periods of childbirth and apprenticeship for the role of household mistress, assumption of the mistress role, and acquisition of daughters-in-law and grandchildren. The acquisition of grandchildren initiated anticipatory socialization for retirement which followed the complete relinquishment of the role of the household mistress (Harvey, 1979).

In traditional Korean society a woman's normative role was difficult to satisfy because it was based on unrealistic expectations and overwhelming tasks where there could be little argument. Korean women married and continued to marry commandants rather than men. Even in Korea today, the husband and his family have rights and privileges while the wife has obligations.

Female role socialization focused more on acquisition of skills in specifically female tasks, accompanied by increased restrictions of movement and closer supervision. In families sufficiently affluent to dispense with their daughters' labor outside the house, the girls were "locked up inside the gate." As a girl grew up, the family began to actively concern itself with the arrangement of a suitable marriage for her. In the meantime, her female role models imparted to her, ideally, such traditionally adaptive strategies that had worked for them in coping with difficulties generally associated with the domestic role of women. They counseled her that the first law of behavior for women was obedience; the best way to cope with men and persons of authority in general was not by direct confrontation, since women had no authority, but by covert management of the total social situation, including the key actors in it; and the best way to insure personal social security was to become indispensably useful to men regardless of their treatment towards her.

By the time of the third or fourth birthday of a Korean girl, an appropriately socialized girl was expected to know, if only intuitively, that: (1) women are inferior to men and, therefore, she is an inferior being, and any claim she has at the present for preferential treatment rests on her relative immaturity and helplessness alone; (2) she cannot reasonably expect to appeal to, or be treated by, the same system of justice as the male. In situations of conflict between the sexes, men are right by virtue of their maleness while women are wrong by virtue of their sex. (3) Women are peripheral to their social environment and tangential to their men. Consequently, if a woman persists in egocentric behavior, she can only provoke intensified punishment.

Even during the early developmental stage, the socialization process for the female child is not an easy task when male members are present. A mother, who might be inclined to let a child cry out its frustration as a possible technique of discipline, could not do so if it disturbed adult male members present. As disturbances occasioned by girls were less readily tolerated, and girls were more subject to externally cued fluctuations in the care and socialization they received than boys, they tended to be more motivated to develop greater sensitivity, accuracy and vigilance in monitoring the social climate of their environment than boys.

In situations of conflict between sisters and brothers, resolution was usually made in favor of the brothers as a matter of course regardless of their relative ages or issues involved. At best, a girl was cajoled and distracted with substitute consolation "prizes" whether it be mother's breast, being carried on her back, or being taken into the kitchen and given a rare snack. Not infrequently, girls were scolded severely for causing their brothers to feel annoyed without regard to provocations they might have received from their brothers. Also, as a girl child grew more capable of self-locomotion, she learned that there were areas restricted to her but not necessarily to her brothers.

By the time that a girl reached puberty, she should have had a belief in the following concepts: (1) women are inferior to men; (2) women must expect and acquiesce to the preferential treatment accorded males; (3) women are subject to spatial constraints in movements; (4) women must maintain proper social distance from men in their household and practice social avoidance with unrelated men; (5) women must conceal emotions which are incompatible with their role requirements; (6) women must cultivate covert strategies for goal realization, i.e., learn to "work the system"; (7) women are married out to strange households where their reception is uncertain; (8) women who are valued by men and the society are those who uphold cultural values by their conformity and commitment to their female roles, and therein lies the traditionally most reliable social security for women. Since, almost by definition of their role, traditional Korean women were perpetually caught in restricted and unavoidable situations, their adequate and appropriate socialization involved learning to survive through womanhood, without interfering with cultural norms.

Perhaps the single most important lesson to be conveyed to women was that when they entered their husbands' households, they should not, in fact had no right, to demand reciprocal role conformity from others including their husbands. Furthermore, inadequacies or even absence of such reciprocal role conformity did not entitle them to suspend their own role performances. Theirs was not the right to criticize the improper or absent reciprocal behavior of others; theirs was merely the duty to assume, if necessary, a phantom reciprocation of behavior if real reciprocation was lacking and to go on as if they were being reciprocated. In other words, women had to learn that their individuality or personal demands intruded upon their roles only at the terrible risk of self-disclosure and the vulnerability resulting from it. However much their male partners deviated from or failed in the expected performance of their roles, for women to improvise or deviate in their role enactment beyond the culturally permissible range was tantamount to placing one's individuality above one's social utility and accountability to the group. Suppression of self-expression was a key socialization task for Korean women.

What Keeps Women There

In Korean society, women have been the most persecuted single majority group throughout history under feudalistic Confucianism, foreign colonialism, authoritarian patriarchism, and exploitive capitalism. Dong S. Kim (1978) viewed sexism in Korea as a most powerful and original force in the dehumanization process today. The covert and overt degradation, discrimination, and suffering of Korean women are so prevalent that they may have provided an historical and ideological prototype for all aspects of dictatorships, exploitations, and repressions in Korea. He further indicated that the most drastic dehumanization treatment to which many Korean women have been subjected is physical abuse by their husbands.

So why have these issues never been fully discussed? Under the restriction of male-dominant perspectives, we have comfortably evaded the problem as only an issue of women or of a few women (Williams, 1977). Our cultural conditioning has blinded us into regarding Korean women's sufferings as "traditional virtues" or, at most, as "virtues in conflict."

For example, it is culturally inconceivable for women to remain unmarried. Women whose occupational roles forbade them to marry or made it difficult to marry were genuinely pitied and regarded as social non-persons. And once married, women no longer had any legitimate claim on their natal households. The best chances for socially acceptable survival for individual women lay in completely identifying with the interests of their husbands and sons. The surest way for women's self-preservation lay in self-denial. For the majority of women, being forced to deny opportunities in life and to avoid unnecessary challenges was probably frustrating under many circumstances. These frustrations are confronted by many barriers such as educational, legal, and career opportunities.

In recent years, women were not generally denied the benefits of formal education but were discouraged from developing any natural ability or talent which might be used for a career outside the home. "A woman's lack of talent is in itself a virtue," and "If a hen crows, the household crumbles" were frequently used proverbs to check any worldly ambitions of a woman. The result was a general lack of professional skills among women and an incomparably higher percentage of illiteracy among women than among men (Yun, 1975).

Thus women's self-consciousness, buried deep in traditional Korean society, awakened to an awareness of the outside world with the coming of the Western influence of Christianity. The proportion of women in school has increased gradually, but in spite of this quantitative increase, most women students in college study in the departments of Home Economics or the Arts, the so-called "womanly sciences."

The image of women that has been fostered in school does not fit the expected role of women in modern society. The supplementary roles are more emphasized for an ideal woman rather than activity or creativity. School-age girls learn that a good housewife must take care of the household so that her husband can be absorbed into his professional work, and that the love of a woman, who does not expect reward, is compensated by the success and achievement of her husband and children. The ideal image of a woman as "the wise mother and good wife" is admired not only in textbooks, but also in school norms and institutions. "The prize of loyal women," "the prize of great mother," and "the prize of a good housewife" are annually awarded by the government. The idea of "the wise mother and good wife" has been defined as a picture of slavery into which the three traditional virtues of women are obedient wife, self-sacrificing mother, and submissive female. The restricted role of an ideal Korean woman has led to a lack of social consciousness and narrow maternal views (Son, 1978).

In the event of the death of a husband, even though there were no legal prohibitions on remarriage, the custom was to require a widow to remain faithful to her husband and not to remarry (Lee, 1966). If a widow should remarry, she would be considered guilty of an unfilial act against her husband's family. An elaborate system of rewards and punishments was worked out in order to force a value system well designed to create egotism at the expense of normal and healthy lives for women. A special recognition was awarded to women who kept their chastity to the end of their lives after having been widowed in youth, while women who remarried were punished by having all their offspring, generation after generation, barred from government service and thus from respectable society (Rhim, 1978; Lee, 1977).

Such a traditional social restriction is notably prevalent in Korean women's status in terms of social structure. Even though discrimination by sex is forbidden in the Constitution, legal provisions of the Domestic Relation Law entirely ignore this fact. Korean family law carefully regulates the family head succession. The eldest son, who becomes the family head regardless of his age, mental capacity, or own will, gets an additional 50% share of the inheritance besides his share as a son. The married daughter can only inherit 25% of the son's share (Lee, 1981; Son, 1978). If the husband bears a child out of wedlock, he can have this child's name entered in the family register without the agreement of his wife; but in the case of the wife's illegitmate child, it is impossible.

The property which was obtained during the marriage belongs to the husband. At the time of a husband's death, the worth of the wife's domestic labors is not considered at all. Son and Lee also state that in case of divorce, the children are sent to the father, regardless of supporting capability. Korean women used to have no rights in child custody. Therefore, even though a divorced mother raised her child, all the legal rights were governed by her husband (i.e., school registry). Although continuous efforts have been made in promoting women's status in Korea, their position is still a visibly subordinate and oppressed one. Because of their lack of knowledge of the law, many women are deprived of the rights guaranteed by the law and others hesitate to appeal for correction of unjust treatment, in fear of the effect that such an appeal would have on their families. They are still hampered by the traditional concept of a subordinate position for women. Although the status of Korean women is guaranteed by law, many have little knowledge of law, and therefore suffer from infringement of their legal rights. There are laws concerning women, but the laws are not properly enforced (Kim, 1971).

According to the statistics presented by D. S. Son, Korean women tend to work only until marriage or pregnancy. "Pretty single women," and "single women with height 160 cm or over" are frequently and commonly sought in newspaper advertisements to fill clerical positions (Son, 1978). A woman sociologist, Hyoje J. Lee, indicates in her 1989 book, *The Status of Korean Women,* that women in Korea have not been liberated much from the traditional patriarchal burden of homemaker and housewife. According to this norm of "the wise mother and good wife" women are expected to have weak social and professional responsibilities (Lee; Kim, 1976).

D. S. Son further explains that Korean women are usually supposed to leave their profession or job early enough not to be called unfortunate women. Married women are also forced to leave their jobs because of spinster preferentialism. A few exceptional women have taken to the difficult road of education and a career, later emerging as prominent national leaders. Except for these pioneers, having a career almost invariably meant renunciation of marriage and family life--the only kind of life other Korean women ever knew.

In order to succeed in the male-oriented Korean society, many women had to become like men, thus once again running against their own nature and becoming alienated from the rest of the female community. It was still not possible for a woman to live and act as an autonomous human being without necessarily disqualifying herself as a woman.

As an example, one woman member of the National Assembly once confessed that women are expected to play the traditional women's role, such as mood setting or assisting in men's affairs, even as an equally professional and publicly elected political Parliament member. So, Ms. O. S. Kim had to disguise herself in male attire in order to not be treated as a woman in the Parliament (Son, 1978). Preference for sons over daughters is still a predominant Korean attitude, and in poor families, education of the daughters is slighted in favor of the less bright sons as a matter of course. Educational material and mass media openly instill the notion of inequality between the sexes by insisting upon highly conventionalized role differentiation. Although women have votes in the majority of instances, they cast their ballots in accordance with their husbands' wishes.

Women of Korea have never been regarded as autonomous human beings but only as appendages to the male members of the family. The only identity a woman had was as someone's daughter, wife, or mother, and she could live her life only through her father, husband, or son (Lee, 1977). Even today, this situation remains largely unchanged in Korean society. Men are legally and socially bestowed authorities with all rights in family affairs. Women have always had an inferior status to that of men, serving primarily as child-bearers and child-carers in the system (Kim, 1976). In such a cultural context, like all Koreans, women maintained surprisingly strong ties with the past. It may be true that Korea, as a developing country, has gone through tremendous social changes in the past two decades, marked by rapid urbanization and the incorporation of Western ideology. These changes have helped break some of the patriarchal family system into an enhanced status of women. This synthesis thus leaves the impression of an uneven course in the history of the Korean women; yet, it has confused and weakened the family structure and relationship in the highly discriminatory and exploitive system.

In the present century, the status of women has probably undergone more changes than that of any other time. As the Koreans' ideal of womanhood changed in accordance with their own rapid modernization, socialization for women was also modified to accommodate these changing expectations. Increasingly, their socialization proceeded on a dual-track course. That is, they were simultaneously socialized on two seemingly contradictory courses: (1) they were socialized in the traditional patterns, almost more rigorously than before to keep the traditional patterns from eroding in the face of many new, competing patterns, and (2) they were socialized in such emergent patterns as seemed to produce the attributes demanded by the more desirable bachelors, although it was done in an ornamental fashion (Harvey, 1980). The Korean society today is undergoing a stage of transition as the old social norms break down without clearly discerning new values to replace them. The rising tide of violence in the family and sexual discrimination practices have become increasing pressures on alienated, vulnerable women since there is an almost total absence of social service provisions in the "modernizing" Korean society. In spite of some gains in recent years, Korean women's social and economic activities and achievements are still seriously curtailed and consistently repressed by Korean society (Song, 1992). Just like in many other developing countries, the issue of wife abuse, or any women-related abuse, does not seem serious enough to warrant concerted external attention. In Korean society, the theorists and activists for improving women's living conditions are composed of just a few groups, and their rare appearances and modest claims suffer from socio-cultural criticism and pressures.

If a hen crows, the household crumbles.

Korean Proverb

CHAPTER 3

How Cultural Conflict Affects Wife Abuse

Experience in a New Land

Immigration affects all of us because the history of the United States is based upon the hardships and accomplishments of people who have immigrated here for political, religious, and economic reasons. Since the revision of the United States Immigration Law in 1965, which eliminated the restriction of the national origin quota system, the rate of Korean immigrants admitted to the country has accelerated (United States Department of Justice, 1970-1976). According to the 1980 census report, Asian-Americans number about 3.5 million. Among the Asian-Americans, the number of Korean immigrants increased 1300 percent between 1965-1974 (Kim, 1976), and it has exceeded 30,000 every year since (Yu, 1980a, 1990).

The total number of Koreans in the United States today is approximately 1,000,000 (*The Korean Times*, S.F., 4/6/1993). The recent Korean immigrants are in their reproductive years, and their children have also contributed to the rapid increase of the Korean population in this country. In terms of age and sex distribution, the majority of new immigrants from Asia are young and female (Hurh and Kim, 1984). Hurh and Kim (1984) indicate that the overall sex ratio of Korean immigrants was 64 males for 100 females in 1977 as compared with 92/100 for the Chinese, 68/100 for the Filipino immigrants, and 95/100 for the United States national population in the same year.

Newcomers make up the majority of Koreans in the United States, although their immigration to America dates back to 1903 - 1905 when a little over 7,000 Koreans went to Hawaii to work on the sugar plantations and intended to stay for temporary labor (Shin, 1978). The first groups of people who immigrated to Hawaii were mostly of lower socio-economic strata, often penniless and uneducated, who found living in Korea unbearable (Harvey, 1980). The next group of Korean immigrants admitted to the United States, up until 1965, was composed of students and Korean women who were married to American servicemen and war orphans adopted by American families (Kim, D.S., 1978). Since the Immigration Act of 1965, Korean immigrants have been one of the largest groups entering the United States, and their rate of increase has been more drastic than any other immigrant group from Asia.

In contrast to the first arrivals in 1903, a majority of recent Korean immigrants seem to agree that they were not indigent or poverty stricken, but felt they voluntarily came out of Korea. Many recent immigrants came to the United States not so much for survival, but rather to elevate their individual socio-economic status, for political stability, and to improve educational opportunity for their children (Kim, D.S., 1978). Unlike their uneducated predecessors, the new Korean immigrants are relatively well educated. Prior to their immigration from Korea, a high proportion of the Korean adult immigrants had already received four years of college education or more and held white-collar occupations (Hurh and Kim, 1984).

Although Korean immigrants seem to be more dispersed geographically than other Asian immigrants, the substantial majority of them are concentrated in metropolitan areas such as Los Angeles, New York, Honolulu, and Chicago. According to a study (Hong and Shin, 1975), more than 90 percent of the Koreans live in urban areas. In Los Angeles, New York, and Chicago, areas where Korean shops are concentrated have been named "Korean-town" by the Koreans.

These Korean-towns give an impression that Koreans tend to concentrate in a few selected areas of the United States (Yu, 1980, *Koreans in America: Dreams and Realities*).

Due to the recentness of their immigration, Koreans in the United States are largely foreign-born, young, and Korean-speaking. Adult Koreans are predominantly Korean-born. Korean immigrants seem to agree that they also came to the United States to better their lives. Regardless of their background, few were prepared for life in the United States. In reality, Korean immigrants experience tremendous differences between two cultures which often result in frustration and miscommunication. One may wonder how the Korean immigrant families adjust themselves to the American way of life. More specifically, one might be curious about the differential patterns of cultural and social adjustment among the recent Korean immigrant families. Although recently increasing in number, relatively little research has been done on the Korean immigrants in the United States, as compared to studies on Japanese and Chinese Americans (Kitano and Stanley, 1973).

Bok Lim C. Kim (1978) completed a comprehensive needs assessment of Asian-Americans in the Chicago area. The study indicated similarities and differences in needs among different Asian groups (Chinese, Japanese, Korean, and Filipino). She also, in her appraisal of Korean immigrant service needs, found that the types of problems encountered by the Koreans in America included financial difficulties, family relations, immigrant status change, family separation, underemployment, physical illness, and psychiatric illness (Kim, Y. C., 1976). Several research studies have been done on the Korean churches and communities (Kim & Kim & Hurh, 1979; Lee, 1979; Kim, H.C., 1978; Kwon, 1975): they viewed the Korean church as an agency for the cultural assimilation of Koreans in the United States.

Daniel Lee conducted research on the Korean wives of American servicemen (Lee, 1980). The carefully designed study on both the Korean wives and American husbands produced the profile of American-Korean military transcultural marriage. One of the major findings indicates that there are differences between the strength and strain groups in age composition, level of intercultural competency, religious compatibility, congruency of role expectation, social integration, and problem-solving mechanisms. Lee also indicates that most Korean wives suffer from language problems and feelings of isolation and separation. Further cultural differences also created psychological distance between couples. Some experience anxiety associated with social prejudice and stress associated with child rearing because of their language and cultural barriers with American child rearing practices. The lack of supportive systems coupled with limited mobility have profound implications for both their participation in the mainstream of American life and their crisis management.

A previous nationwide study by Dong-Soo Kim is the study of the self-concept of adopted Korean adolescents (Kim, 1977). The result of the study shows that the Korean adopted children had relatively little Korean identity. As a whole, they had remarkably similar self-concepts to that of other Americans as represented by a norm group. A supportive family environment did tend to promote a better self-concept formulation among the adopted Korean children. There is another study of American-born children and their Korean-born parents. Kwang-Lim Koh and Hesung C. Koh had made a summary of three conferences of Koreans, discussing the problems of the first generation of Korean parents and their American-born children (Koh and Koh, 1974).

Kim, E. (1990) identifies their major problems as characterized by cultural differences, lack of education, impoverishment, isolation, miscommunication in the family, and narrow job opportunities which have severe bearings on their acculturation and assimilation processes. Since the essence of culture is language, both written and oral communication, it is found that the majority of Korean immigrants experience a great deal of difficulty with the English language (98% of Koreans surveyed were using Korean as their primary language) which affects their adjustments to American society and intrafamiliar communication (Schnepp and Yu, 1955; Lee, 1975). Kim and others report that this very language deficiency is directly associated with many other problems. Yu also indicated that language is a major obstacle for Koreans in the process of making a new life in the United States (Yu, 1990). Language barriers notwithstanding, Koreans are eager for full participation in their new society: Half of the Korean immigrants obtain American citizenship within six years of arrival, the highest rate among Asian subgroups (Kim, Hyun-Chan, 1977).

The language difficulty of Koreans severely limits their cultural and social activities. They are generally Korean-directed in their cultural activities, relying mostly on Korean newspapers for general information affecting their daily lives. In other words, a majority of Koreans learn about American life and society through Korean newspapers. Group and organizational activities of the Koreans tend to be Korean-centered. They attend Korean churches and participate in the activities of Korean organizations. There are over three hundred Korean churches in Southern California that conduct most of their affairs only in Korean (*Han-Kook Daily News*, 4/21/83:9).

The 1978 Chicago survey of 116 Korean blue-collar workers shows that none of the respondents reported membership in American voluntary associations, while most of them were affiliated with Korean ethnic organizations such as churches and alumni associations (Hurh, Kim, and Kim, 1979). Koreans may be fully assimilated to American culture, but they nevertheless will be forced to remain outside the inner social circle of the white majority. McWilliams (1964) viewed that the systematic legal, economic, and social discriminatory practices against immigrants and their descendants have successfully limited the numbers of immigrants, opportunities for economic advancement, housing mobility, and the social integration of the immigrants into the fabric of American life. Bogardus (1968) has demonstrated that the American people want even less (primary level) association with Koreans than with other Asian groups. Hurh, Kim, and Kim (1979) argue that Koreans as an ethnic group seem to be accorded an extremely low social prestige by Americans in general, and their data seem to support their contention.

Given the circumstances described above, it appears clearly that Korean immigrants are going through a critical experience in the adjustment process, especially for those who are relatively new to the United States and who have family members. This results in family disharmony, self and family crises, and despair. Thus, recent Korean immigrants face the family problems which arise from the different viewpoints of the new land.

When Old Cultures Break Down

One might conclude that many of the factors which contributed to the incidence of wife beating in traditional Korean families are no longer present because of the rapid and successful adjustment to American culture of Korean immigrants from the superficial perspective. Nevertheless, it is possible to identify some of the factors contributing to wife abuse in Korean immigrant families during their cultural adaptation process. Three factors will be identified in the following discussion: (1) attitude toward traditionalism (cultural accepting factors); (2) adherence to rigid sex role; and (3) stress-evoking factors (e.g., status inconsistency, language, and cultural barriers).

Attitude toward traditionalism

It should be noted that American and Korean values are based on different standards. Basic American cultural values often conflict with Korean values. The fundamental American value structure is an individual-oriented one, while the Korean is interpersonal or communal. The doctrine of the relationships, the cornerstone of all Korean Confucian moral and social teaching, begins with the concept of clear distinction and proper order between husband and wife. Based on this understanding of the cultural difference between the two value systems, the Korean immigrant family situation may be viewed more clearly (see Table 1).

Wife abuse may have been a result in certain societies or groups because it is understood to be a culturally accepted aspect of husband-wife interactions (Stark and McEvoy, 1970; Wolfgang and Ferracuti, 1967). The cultural norms and values appear to be more important in the analysis of wife abuse in Korean immigrant families than in white American families. To determine the importance of Korean cultural tradition which is contributing to the incidence of wife abuse, we have to evaluate the ways in which cultural factors influence both family interaction and the likelihood of violence in the family.

In studying the causes of violence in Korean immigrant families, we need to consider that it has been tolerated in traditional Korean society. If we take an example from Korean traditional proverbs, the husband's mother had encouraged her son to beat his wife once in a while when it was needed, to remind her of the duties of a "good" Korean wife. Any Korean wife who is bold enough to behave in a way which is not proper from the standpoint of the role traditionally assigned to her deserves any treatment that she gets from her husband. This phenomenon was also found to be practiced in Korean immigrant families in studies from the files of the Korean American Mental Health Center in Los Angeles (Yim, 1978). Yim further indicated that a wife's violation of traditional norms is viewed as being serious enough to warrant any means, including violence, to bring about conformity to these norms. Since the cultural norms legitimize the use of violence in the family, then such violence can be considered to be normal and accepted. Korean immigrants bring with them the traditional acceptance of wife abuse as a way of coping with marital conflict. Many Korean battered women tend to hold traditional, accepting attitudes regarding appropriate husband-wife interaction. The old image of ideal womanhood is submissive, nonassertive, and obedient to whatever the husband's life offers.

Thus, Korean immigrants have to deal with two sets of values which guide and direct their marriage--the Korean tradition on the one hand, and the American value system on the other. While there are many cultural elements which can be complementary between these two sets of cultures, they are often contradictory and create marital conflicts.

Though the Korean immigrant wife may accept traditional viewpoints in regard to abuse, serious conflicts are likely to arise when the husband seeks to retain traditional values pertaining to husband-wife relations, this occurring at the same time the wife is starting to openly question these values and adopt American cultural norms. This gap between the two cultural patterns may become a cause of marital conflict, leading to violence in Korean immigrant families.

Adherence to rigid sex role

One of the most salient characteristics of wife-beaters is their strict adherence to a rigidly defined male role. This compulsive masculinity is reflected in an attempt to maintain total dominance over their wives (Davidson, 1978; Martin, 1983; Walker, 1979). The socialization process of assigning male and female sex role behavior is well known as contributing to violence against women (Walker, 1979). While batterers are more rigidly socialized into the male sex role expectation, many battered women also tend to hold stereotypical attitudes regarding appropriate masculine and feminine behavior.

TABLE 1

THE FUNDAMENTAL IDEAS AND VALUES WHICH ARE COMMON IN KOREA BUT DIFFERENT FROM AMERICAN PERSPECTIVE

Dimension	Ideal Korean View	Ideal American View
Human dignity	"human interrelatedness" quality of one's relationships with others	"individualism" independence of thoughts and judgements
Social relationship	reverence for others, proper order in society	self-reliance, creativity, courageous exercise of a responsible freedom
Decorum	proper and polite behavior	informality, casualness
Personal rights and duties	gracious favor	stand up for one's rights
Age	between elder and younger there should be proper order	equality
Male & female	there should be proper distinction	equality
Marriage	to continue the family line	love
Problem solving attitude	endurance	confrontation
Happiness	harmony	individual fulfillment

Source: Kalton, M. (1979); "Korean Ideas and Values"; Kim, J., (1978); "Some Value Questions for Ethnic Orientation"; Hurh, W., and Kim. (1984) *Korean Immigrants in America.*

Korea has traditionally maintained a typical patrilineal family system based on the Confucian philosophy which encompasses a multi-generation of family members through the male line, the relationships among these members being fixed in the framework of the patriarchal system (Lee, 1973). A well-defined set of marital roles are produced by this family system. The family unit is more important than the individual. Decisions are made in favor of the family by the husband, rather than for the sole benefit of a single member. In the Korean family system, a Korean wife is also expected to serve her husband and other members of her husband's family and, finally, to be an instrument in the perpetuation of her husband's family lineage (Choi, 1977). Korean married women are confined to domestic roles in their husbands' families.

The following is an example of how the language reflects the stratification and segregation of the sexes and interpersonal relations in Korean thought. A wife speaks of her husband as "the master of our house," *urichip chuin.* She may refer to him as the "outside gentleman," *pakkat yangban.* In sharp contrast, the wife is the husband's *chip saram* or his *an saram*, "house person" or "inside person" (Crane, 1967). The rigid sex roles of Korean wives still persist in Korea despite sweeping social changes, increased educational opportunities for Korean women, and the rapid progress in industrialization and urbanization of Korea (Kim, D.S., 1978; Kim, 1971; Lee, 1976).

Korean immigrant couples bring with them the traditional stereotypes of husband as superior, strong, aggressive, and authoritarian; in contrast, the wife is portrayed as subordinate, weak, passive, and showing absolute obedience to her husband (Yim, 1978). However, the immigrant Korean's new social and work environment requires certain changes with respect to traditional lifestyles and ways of thinking (see Table 2). Family structures in Korea show the husband and wife having little involvement in activities together at home and elsewhere, and she does not expect to share or exchange many roles. However, in the Korean family unit in the United States, the husband and wife are expected to carry out many activities together with a minimum of differentiation of roles and interests. Therefore, absolute male dominant sex roles in the traditional Korean family cannot be maintained intact in the United States (Yu, 1980, "Demographic Profile of Koreans in Los Angeles: Size, Composition, and Distribution.").

The traditional Korean rigid sex roles are in marked contrast to American family life in terms of ideal husband and wife interaction. Additionally, there is a conflict between Koreans and Americans in the family's role expectations. These gaps between two cultures may become a cause of marital conflict and lead to violence in Korean immigrant families (Yim, 1978). Conflict between the husband and wife arises where the role performance needs to be changed in the context of American culture. When Korean husbands and wives start to disagree about the nature of their respective roles and about new ways of raising children, the husband may try to resolve the resulting conflict by violence against his wife.

In Korea, there is a clear distinction between the roles of wives and husbands. The roles of driver, cook, baby sitter, and shopper are rarely performed by the husband in Korea. The majority of Koreans use public transportation; cooking is done by the wife or housemaid, and baby-sitting is done only by females. For instance, the kitchen, which in Korea is off-limits to men under normal circumstances, intrudes conspicuously in the United States home structure into the living room, which must be shared by all members of the family. These types of arrangements are apparently more distressing to the men, not only because they have had less experience than women in intense domestic environments, but also because these changes come at a time when they feel extremely vulnerable from the cultural transition.

These conflicts seem to arise because of living in a new culture. The conflicts both sexes recognize are closely related to

TABLE 2

ROLE CONFLICTS FACED BY RECENT KOREAN IMMIGRANT FAMILY MEMBERS IN A FOREIGN CULTURE

Role Dimension	Wife	Husband
Full time management of household and child rearing	now full time working wife	housework must be shared by all members of the family
Financially, emotionally fully dependent	independent power	losing man - over -woman domination
Obedient attitude toward husband	becomes assertive	feelings of helplessness resulting in depression

Children	Parents
See more freedom of choice and become independent more quickly in America than they did in Korea	Find their children become more uncontrollable (Thus the frustration is doubled especially for those whose immigration motive was their "children's education")
Recognize that their parents' attitudes toward them are quite authoritarian as compared to parents of their local friends	
Adjust to the new culture much faster than their parents, rapidly arriving at the level of social interaction, American value system	Still in the period of adjustment or at the level of long-term cultural assimilation

The equal rights among members of family and gradeless (nonhonorific) speech found in American society may cause disharmony in Korean immigrant families.

Source: Kalton, M. (1979); Song (1990)

each other. For example in the United States, domestic affairs cannot be handled by wives alone and they need help from husbands. On the other hand, husbands alone cannot solve external problems because wives are involved in socio-economic matters. Therefore, most of the decision-making has to be done jointly.

In the Korean traditional point of view, the woman's role should be limited to giving helpful advice; she should never take over the role of decision-maker. The high economic participation rate among Korean immigrant women weakens the male-dominant role of the traditional family. As wives become partners in economic activity, they no longer obediently accept the superior position of males. In this respect, the husband feels no absolute dominance over his wife, but often he expects and forces his wife to behave as if she were in Korea. This usually enrages the husband, who will then resort to violence. Even though the Korean immigrant wife may accept the traditional definition of her role, the influence of American culture could easily make her aware of the fact that an American husband is expected to share sex roles. Thus, when she feels particularly overburdened with absolute demands of the Korean wife's role, she may ask her husband to change. This request may upset each partner. Similarly, as the wife becomes aware of American patterns of child-rearing, she could become dissatisfied with the authoritarianism of her husband. If she expresses her disagreement, this also could lead to conflicts that may lead to abuse (Yim, 1978).

At the same time, Korean husbands tend to resist the transition and stick to the old authoritarian controls over their wives and children. Consequently, conflicts between parent and child intensify marital conflict (Hurh, 1977). Under these circumstances, it is difficult to maintain a stable child-parent, husband-wife relationship.

The high economic participation rate among Korean women, like other immigrant wives in the American history of immigration (Chafe, 1976), weakens the male-dominant role of the traditional husband. Korean immigrant wives are employed to support their family because the earnings of their husbands are usually not sufficient to meet all of the family needs (Hurh and Kim, 1984). Disadvantages in the American labor market are another reason for the high labor force participation rate of Korean married women, and a high proportion of Korean husbands turn to self-employed small businesses such as laundromats, Korean restaurants and stores, etc. (Min, 1988; Kim and Hurh, 1983; Wong and Hirschman, 1983). Management of such small businesses is difficult enough to require the labor of unpaid family members to cut down the cost. Most of the employed wives are working particularly long hours.

Under these circumstances, do their husbands share the role of homemaker in their families? It has been observed that the immigrant wives alone are expected to perform most of the household tasks, regardless of their employment status or the presence of children. In this respect, Korean immigrant husbands and wives reveal that the immigrant wives are no less traditional than the husbands. When both immigrant husbands and wives continue to believe that the wife should predominantly perform household tasks regardless of the situation, the combination of the extended full-time employment and responsibility for most of the household tasks would mean that the working wives suffer from the heavy burden of their double roles. Eventually, the wives would feel an acute sense of injustice or inequity (Hurh and Kim, 1984).

The Korean immigrant wives begin to question, and they no longer obediently and fully accept the superior position of their husbands. Husbands who are already faced with frustration caused by language difficulties, prejudice, and discrimination in the employment market find it difficult to tolerate their weakening position in the family (Kim, H.C., 1977). Husbands feel helpless when seeing their authority over their wife and children erode. Anger, thus accumulated, explodes between husbands and wives.

However, in Korean immigrant families, there is little possibility of role sharing or interchange between the wives and their husbands. Korean immigrant couples continue to exhibit sharp sex role segregation. Overburdened Korean immigrant wives and their frustrated husbands face the problems concerning "family violence" which are coupled with the different viewpoints in the new culture. It leaves them extremely vulnerable.

Stress-evoking factors

There is considerable evidence to indicate that situational stresses affect the level of wife abuse. For instance, unemployment, job dissatisfaction, and financial difficulties are frequently associated with episodes of battering (Gelles, 1972; Prescott & Letko, 1977; Roy, 1977). The stress-evoking environments are focused on the implications of sociological, cultural, and economic difficulties in addition to family structure and interaction. One would expect that families which have little status, power, or money have to resort to violence as the "resource" available to relieve their frustrations and stresses (Goode, 1974).

At any socio-economic level, however, the stages of the family cycle, as well as extended family relations, are related to violence between husband and wife. We need to consider the discrepancies or inconsistencies between the socio-economic achievements of husbands and wives and between family socio-economic backgrounds and current status of husbands. For example, a study indicates that family violence tends to occur more often when the wife was earning more money than her spouse (O'Brien, 1971).

Despite high pre-immigration socio-economic status, most Korean immigrants are employed under relatively unfavorable labor market conditions in the United States. Upon arrival in the United States, the majority of the recent immigrants from Korea start their occupational careers as low-skilled blue collar or service workers, and eventually a high proportion of them become small business entrepreneurs (Hurh and Kim, 1984; Kim and Hurh, 1983). Especially for Koreans in America, an important element of stress is the combination of unsatisfactory occupational status, which includes unemployed husbands and wives working outside the home. While Korean men have very high educational levels, their occupational and income levels tend to be much lower than could be expected from their education. Many college graduates have blue-collar jobs, and due to discrimination in licensing, many Korean professionals are either unemployed and underemployed or have non-professional jobs. While both unemployment or underemployment may cause frustrations and stresses leading to violence, the impact of these conditions on marital relations and violence is seen in the Korean immigrant families (Yim, 1978).

Yim further explained that couples who had their marriages arranged in Korea and who lived with their parents had developed a pattern of adjustment that did not require intense interaction between them. For their marriage to be successful in the traditional sense, there was no need for them to get to know each other. For the first time, husband and wife may be by themselves without any other extended family members and thus may have to face each other every day. Consequently, problems they did not experience in Korea may surface and have to be confronted. This can cause intense stress, and wife abuse becomes one of the responses to that stress.

Conjugal violence is sometimes the result of stress from cultural shock. Due to the complete lack of research in this area, empirical data has not been developed. However, the closest approach applicable concerning cultural loss could be compared to the crisis reaction. There have been some systematic attempts to describe the human experience of crisis from the loss caused by transition. Fink (1967) and Parkes (1972) have described some of the stages that people pass through in coping with bereavement. Mead and MacGregor (1951) examined the effects of change on traditional stable cultures.

Kim (1976) explained that the immigration process signifies disruption and disintegration of a familiar lifestyle. It involves disintegration of the person's intra-familial relationships, loss of social identity, and major shifts in the value system and behavior patterns. It is an upheaval and disequilibrium of catastrophic proportions which can be considered a crisis. For immigrant Korean couples, the process is fraught with danger, and it challenges all their resources in order to cope with this crisis. It frequently places the marital relationship in a most vulnerable state which may lead to violence in the family.

Stress due to the culture shock may be an experience of a sudden trauma arising from disorientation, displacement, disappointment, alienation, loneliness, a feeling of total inadequacy, cognitive dissonance, and loss of self-control during the cultural transition crisis.

A study by Hurh, Kim, and Kim (1979) examines the recent Korean immigrants in terms of their adaptation process in the United States. Hurh proposed a model of adaptation process based on the six critical phases that most Korean immigrants are undergoing. This model of the psychological adaptation process, as measured by the length of sojourn and the degree of life satisfaction, suggests six phases which can be explicated as follows: (1) the first phase is the exuberant period of the initial months after the immigrants arrive in the United States when they experience feelings of exuberance, accomplishment and relief that they have finally "made it" safely to the new country. (2) This elated feeling will soon be followed by a period of "cultural shock" approximately within the first year of adaptation. The immigrants' dream begins to fade when they are confronted with the harsh realities of a language barrier, unemployment, and social isolation. At this stage, the immigrant will most likely doubt if he can "make it." He may regret that he left home for a strange land and yearn to return to his homeland. Hurh views this cultural shock as a form of anxiety, which results from the loss of perceptual reinforcements from one's own culture to new cues that have no meaning at all, little meaning, or a meaning different from those in the homeland. (3) As time goes on, "adjustment" begins, and cultural shock is redressed through this experience in the American lifestyle. (4) After five to seven years, the immigrant continues to improve his life conditions and reaches an optimum phase. (5) After going through the optimum period of satisfaction, the immigrants are again faced with another set of critical phase-identification crises: Korean immigrants experience feelings of relative deprivation and a perception of limited assimilation. Despite the high level of assimilation, the immigrant tends to experience an increased sense of status inconsistency and discrimination. (6) The immigrants arrive at the final phase of "acceptance" when they maintain neutral, marginal satisfaction.

Acceptance of an unwelcome reality is a defense mechanism, a reaction to a serious threat. The abhorrence of impending deprivation, disappointment, and the threat of serious cultural loss is changed at times into acceptance. At this phase, they have neither expectations nor aspirations for "success" in their immigration lives: they simply survive. Overall, the six transition phases represent a cycle of experiencing a disruption, then gradually acknowledging its reality, testing oneself, and understanding oneself.

Interestingly, Elisabeth Kubler-Ross (1975) has also introduced a similar curve of a reaction cycle that people go through upon learning they are terminally ill--the ultimate transition as crisis. Immigration, whether motivated by the search for a better life or flight from political or economic hardships, results in intermingled emotions of grief, anger, loneliness, guilt, and shame as we find in the crisis reaction introduced by Kubler-Ross. The process of adaptation could be compared to the crisis in cultural loss. Conjugal violence is often the result of such crisis reactions as vulnerability.

Being a Victim

While those self-centered social activities which were mentioned in the previous discussion may help preserve cultural traditions, they tend to enforce culturally social isolation. On a superficial level, Korean immigrants seem to adjust well to the new culture. However, more serious domestic problems arise between the Korean immigrant couple in the process of adjustment to a new cultural setting.

A recent report by staffs at Korean counseling service centers in the Chicago area indicates the seriousness of wife abuse among Korean families. According to that report, wife abuse appears to be a more serious problem among Korean immigrant families than any other domestic problem. Also, the number of incidents has been rapidly increasing as the Korean immigrant population increases. At the same time, most of the battered Korean women are ignorant about available services. They tend to wait until they are seriously hurt before inquiring about possible services. The report also indicates that each caseworker at the centers deals with a large number of battered women, wife abuse being the most prevalent problem faced by Korean immigrant women (*The Korean Times*, 9/20/85).

Overall, adjustment difficulties experienced by the Korean immigrants have serious implications for violence in the families as they undergo acculturation in the United States. Many of the Korean immigrants throughout the United States showed evidence that they have failed to cope with the various problems in living in America (Song, 1991). Song argued that mental health problems such as mental and emotional stress, the language barrier, employment problems, insecurity of living conditions, and environmental changes have caused serious marital problems beyond observation and estimation.

In addition, another difficulty in aiding domestic violence among Koreans are their unique characteristics and capacity to control expressions of problems and troubles. Acknowledgment of an emotional disturbance is seen as a sign of personal inadequacy which reflects poorly on the individual and the family. The consensus of American people is that Asians have strong family ties. It is thought that by segregating themselves in the larger society, Asians are insulated against the stresses, anxieties, and problems of life. There is also a widespread belief that Asian-Americans have somehow overcome prejudice and therefore do not require special attention and aid. Contrary to these beliefs that Asians are model citizens with low stress and low maladjustment, several research reports indicate that Asian populations are actually more vulnerable than many other population groups (Kitano, 1967; Tung, 1980; Ishisaka and Takagi, 1982; Dhooper and Tran, 1986). Studies of Asian populations in America have discovered not only serious problems but also a marked underutilization of available social services and facilities by them (Lorenzo and Adler, 1984; Sue and McKinney, 1975; Mokuau and Matsuoka, 1986).

Most Korean immigrants stress privacy and self-control, and their view of battering in the home environment may encourage them to try to solve the problem on their own without letting close friends know. Stigma and shame may be felt by a woman who experiences battering. The battered Korean woman may not seek help because of the anticipated disgrace of the need to go out of the family. The view traditionally is that the capacity to control expressions of family problems or troubled feelings is equated with maturity, and they hesitate to seek any formal help. Thus, most Koreans regard domestic problems as sources of potential danger and of shame to their families.

Koreans rarely regard their problems, including psychosomatic symptoms, as serious if they are not acted out in ways dangerous to others. Many Asians tend to somatize their problems by attributing them to a "headache" or "indigestion" rather than to a psychological reaction such as anxiety (Ponce, 1974: Chung and Rieckelman, 1974). A Korean psychiatrist (Chung, 1980) indicated that as long as persons lead calm, withdrawn lives, domestic problems are well tolerated by both the family and the society. Among Korean women, the most common type of problem is the paranoid type. This symptom is on the increase in Korean women, perhaps owing to traditional repression of verbalization and emotional expression. Depression is becoming more common, especially in situations involving accumulated fear toward violent husbands. However, due to the unfamiliarity and cultural barriers in counseling, they generally seek relief from Korean internists (Chung, 1980).

One of the reasons for the immigrant population to seek help from ethnic medical professionals is that American service providers may not be responsive and sensitive to the client's fears, beliefs, and perspectives on life and situations (Dhooper and Tran, 1986). At the same time, formal services based on Anglo-American culture may appear to be irrelevant to their perceived problems, confusing, and possibly stigmatizing to them (Ryan, 1976). Unfamiliarity with the nature of counseling also results in underutilization of services. They either do not seek help or they drop out of the counseling programs.

There is abundant evidence that came to light in the 1970's that public services were being underutilized by minority groups and that behavior described as pathological in a minority culture such as individualistic assertiveness may be viewed as adaptive in a majority culture client (Murphy, 1978). Asian-Americans terminate counseling significantly earlier than Anglo clients (Sue and McKinney, 1975). In most of the literature these examples of differentiation are credited to cultural barriers that hinder the formation of good counseling relationships, language barriers, class-bound values, and culture-bound attitudes.

Bok-Lim Kim (1978) also explained that immigrants not only have to face new and unfamiliar situations, but they also encounter institutional and individual racism which makes their adjustment even more difficult. She argued that it may be possible to mobilize one's inner strengths to cope with unfamiliar situations, but it is often impossible to cope with a system which does not allow one to succeed because of discriminatory practices. Therefore, the immigrants have to be taught that some of their failures might be due to their own inabilities to deal with unfamiliar or difficult situations, while other situations might be beyond resolution because of institutional failure (Kim, 1976).

Amir (1969) reviewed the literature of social psychology from minority perspectives in a classic article on contact under unfavorable conditions, and he concluded that intergroup contact results in more negative relationships and disharmony. These unfavorable conditions are most easily illustrated in the relationships between dominant and minority groups. Sue and McKinney (1975) include the condition of being oppressed as an important defining characteristic of any minority group. Minorities, then, are people singled out for unequal and different services and who regard themselves as objects of discrimination. Sue and McKinney (1975) have pointed out how the perception of equality has politicized the delivery of public services in our domestic social context.

Daniel Lee (1984) indicated in his recent study that Asians are not immune from strains due to the internal and external social realities of cultural alienation and institutional racism. Lee further pointed out that the myth of the "successful minority" is often applied to Asian-Americans who have structurally assimilated into the mainstream of American society, while it negates categorically a large segment of the same ethnic population whose survival needs and ethnic barriers hamper their access to equal opportunities. Asian-Americans, including Koreans, tend to underutilize public services and counseling for problem-solving and conflict management of life crises. Often they mask difficulties because it is considered shameful to show weakness; disgrace to the family and ancestors is felt to be sinful (Lee, 1984).

CHAPTER 4

Theories on Wife Abuse

Theories concerning wife abuse are based primarily in sociological theories of family violence and psychological theories of aggression which have been used to explain violence against wives. These theories tend to be broad, and few are mutually exclusive. As specialization increases, we reach the point where some significant questions have to be answered that cannot be answered satisfactorily within the sociological or psychological framework.Though social-psychological theories progress beyond intra-individual explanations, they still fail to provide a full explanation for wife abuse. Consideration of the large society--the context in which the relationship takes place--is characteristic only of socio-cultural perspectives (Thoennes, 1981). The socio-cultural approach is based on the assumption that violence cannot be effectively studied in isolation from the values, norms and structure of the society (Straus, 1976, 1977). Hence, wife abuse must be viewed in terms of the cultural context from which it springs. It is suggested that the perspective of a sociocultural approach is a three-stage model which requires the integration of the sociological and psychological components. This provides an additional aspect to the dual perspective (see Figure 1).

This three-stage model, as proposed by Hoyos, Hoyos, and Anderson (1986), is based on a continuum designed to assess minority battered women at the individual level, as they

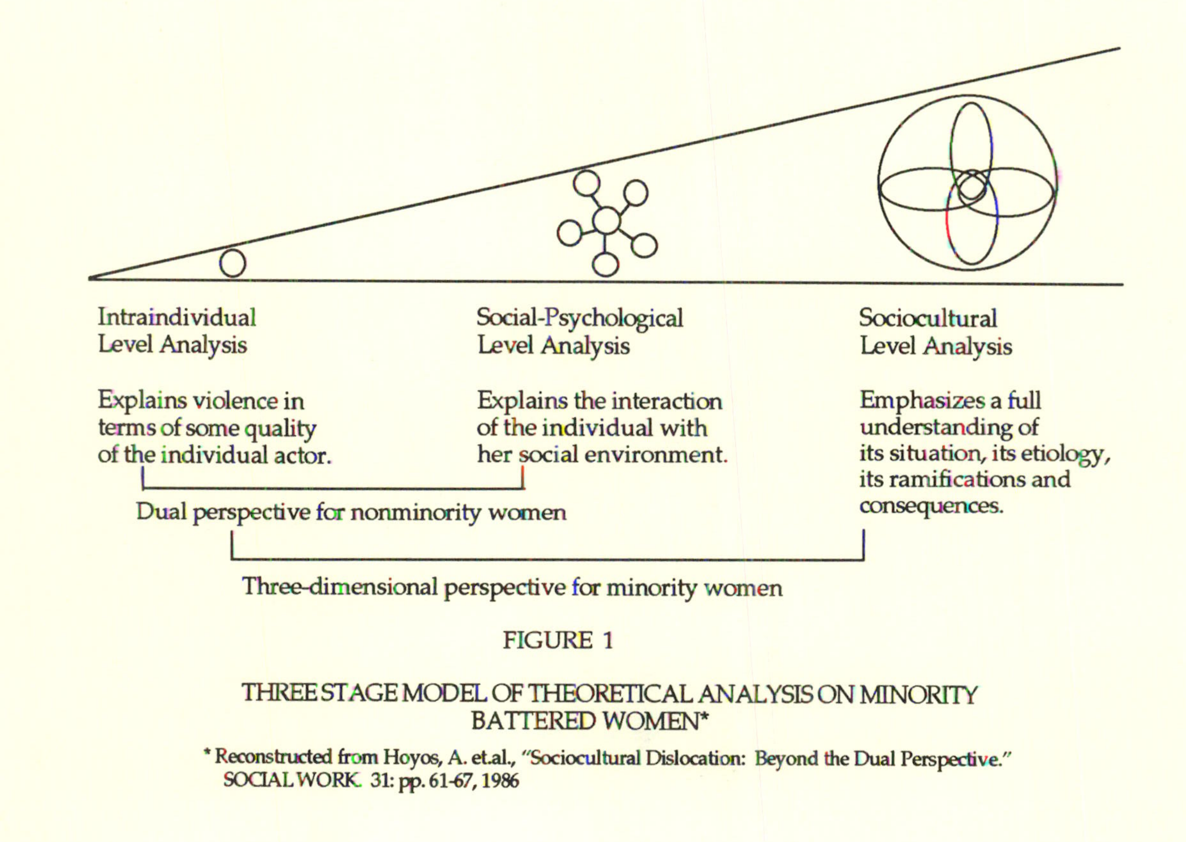

FIGURE 1

THREE STAGE MODEL OF THEORETICAL ANALYSIS ON MINORITY BATTERED WOMEN*

* Reconstructed from Hoyos, A. et.al., "Sociocultural Dislocation: Beyond the Dual Perspective." SOCIAL WORK. 31: pp. 61-67, 1986

interact within their support systems, and as they perform their roles in societal structures. An emphasis will be placed on the major sociocultural theoretical formulation of a culture-of-violence approach pertaining to the question of why battering occurs.

Culture-of-Violence Theory

This theory contends that violence is unevenly distributed in the subcultures. The difference in ideas and attitudes toward violence can be observed through variables unrelated to social class such as ethnicity. The culture-of-violence theory explains violence as part of a subcultural normative system which is reflected in the subculture participants (Palmer, 1962; Wolfgang, 1958; Wolfgang and Ferracuti, 1967). The term subculture refers to transmitted and created content and patterns of values. It incorporates ideas or a complex symbolic, meaningful system which includes all of the following: morals, beliefs, attitudes, knowledge, laws, habits, standards, customs, rituals as factors in the shaping of human behavior, and the artifacts produced through behavior which distinguishes it from the dominant culture. The concept of the culture-of-violence further suggests that there is a potent theme of violence current in the cluster of values that makes up the lifestyle, the socialization process, and the interpersonal relationships of individuals living in similar environments (Wolfgang and Ferracuti, 1967).

Violent behavior can be considered as a production of the essential core of culture which consists of traditional ideas and their attached values. The normative concept of culture in the culture-of-violence theory requires viewing norms as cultural, not by virtue of being norms, but only in so far as they define violent responses as normative rather than deviant. As such, the overt use of violence in interpersonal relationships is generally viewed as a reflection of basic values that stand apart from the central, or the parent culture (Wolfgang and Ferracuti, 1967).

In light of this discussion, caution is to be exercised in the interpretive analysis of the culture-of-violence theory. Wolfgang and Ferracuti offered an explanation as follows (1967, pp. 158-161): (1) no subculture can be totally different from or totally in conflict with the society of which it is a part; (2) to establish the existence of a subculture of violence does not require that the actors sharing in these basic value elements should express violence in all situations; (3) the potential resort or willingness to resort to violence in a variety of situations emphasizes the penetrating and diffusive character of this culture theme; (4) the subcultural ethos of violence may be shared by all ages in a subsociety, but this ethos is most prominent in a limited age group, ranging from late adolescence to middle age; (5) the counter-norm is non-violence; (6) the development of favorable attitudes toward, and the use of, violence in a subculture usually involves learned behavior and a process of differential learning, association, or identification; (7) the use of violence in a subculture is not necessarily viewed as illicit conduct and the users therefore do not have to deal with feelings of guilt about their aggression. Violence can become part of the lifestyle and used mostly between persons and groups who themselves rely upon the same supportive values and norms.

In applying the culture-of-violence theory to violence in the Korean family, several issues arise relative to how wife abuse occurs. Violent acts may have become a part of the lifestyle, the way of solving difficult problems with the Korean family. The battered Korean women who remain in abusive situations might be considered a part of the subculture and view wife abuse as an acceptable and tolerable means of coping with their problems. Battered Korean women further assume an allegiance to their own culture. They have learned to perceive objects, persons, and situations as attractive or threatening, in accordance with subcultural positive and negative factors (Wolfgang and Ferracuti, 1967).

In Korean society, a violent husband will not be burdened by conscious guilt because he is not criticized by the non-violent culture. The recipient of this violence may also be described by similar categories which characterize the subuniverse of the collectivity sharing in the subculture of violence.

On the other hand, the culture-of-violence theory does not explain how the subculture values originate, nor does it explain how these values can be modified or changed over time. In fact, several hypotheses have been advanced to explain the occurrence of violence in some cultures. In the case of Italy, in viewing the outbreaks of spontaneous violence, Wolfgang and Ferracuti (1967) indicated that geographical isolation has certainly contributed to the perpetuation of the violent behavior pattern. Alternative explanations offered include reference to inherited characteristics that fit the known facts about this puzzling area of subculture of violence.

At the same time, it is interesting to note that the geographical situation of Korea is very similar to the situation of Italy. Korea is a country situated on a peninsula which is surrounded by water and a hostile boundary to the north. There is no place to escape from the wrath of an external attack. Like the Italians, whom they are said to resemble, Koreans love music and display an earthy humor, a quick wit, a hot temper, and a strong pride (Crane, 1967). Crane further indicates that the chief factors which have determined traditional Korean patterns of thought and behavior are: geography, which has made Korea a land of extreme external pressure between mighty neighbors; Confucianism, with its emphasis on relationships of the family and reverence for the past and traditional thoughts; and overcrowding, which does not allow for much individualism.

These factors have developed in Korean women an amazing ability to endure; they believe in the submission of an individual for the good of the family. Perhaps there are several ways in different cultural settings in which a subculture of violence arises. It may be that within the same subculture an allegiance to wife abuse may develop into different patterns. For example, wife abuse may occur because of a negative reaction to their own culture, as a positive reaction to a willingness to use negative means, or as a positive absorption of an indigenous set of subcultural values. It should also be noted that there is a conflict of values systems between a prevailing culture value and some subcultural entity.

From this overview based on sociocultural perspectives, we now realize that probably no single theory will ever fully explain the variety of observable wife abuse. However, the culture-of-violence application offers the advantage of bringing together psychological and sociological constructs to aid in understanding the occurrence of violence in specific groups. The conceptualization of a culture-of-violence will be used as a theoretical framework in this study for an integrated sociological and psychological approach. Other relevant theories and data on wife abuse will be introduced in the following discussion in order to provide the systematic analysis that is relevant to our focus on wife abuse, with special emphasis on the culture-of-violence perspective.

Masochist Theory

The alleged masochistic traits of women have been used both as an explanation for battering and as an answer to the question of why battered women stay. It is based on the premise that women remain in an abusive relationship because the battered woman is satisfying a conscious or unconscious need to be dominated and hurt, which is founded on the notion of a biologically determined disposition toward masochism.

Freud proposed that there are two types of masochism: the first is commonly referred to as gaining sexual gratification through physical pain; the second, moral masochism, is derived from sadism which has been turned around and directed against the self (Freud, 1949-50). In "The Economic Problem in Masochism," Freud defined women as innately masochistic and defines masochism as inherently female. In masochism "the subject is placed in a situation characteristic of womanhood, i.e., they mean that he (the subject) is being castrated, is playing the passive role in coitus, or is giving birth" (Freud, 1949-50, p. 258).

The concept of castration, the basis of women's biological inferiority, is a significant determinant of masochistic behavior. Freud specifies that passivity and masochism are interrelated and biologically destined. They are considered the norm of healthy development in females. Generally, the woman's individual problem is believed to be rooted in her childhood experience. Early exposure to abuse, a domineering mother and submissive father, as well as the reverse, have been noted as causal factors (Schultz, 1960; Snell et al., 1964). According to Berlinger (1958), the guilt and punishment experienced by the masochist is a reflection of the need for the love of a person who punishes and makes one feel guilty. Berlinger viewed most masochists as victims of a traumatic childhood and as troublemakers who entangle themselves in conflicts by which they continue to make themselves victims.

In her view of female sexuality, Marie Bonaparte (1965) sustains Freud's theory of biologically based feminine masochism. According to Bonaparte, passivity and masochism are biologically imposed upon the female and, therefore, must be accepted, while the male must protest against the passive attitude since it is not biologically imposed on him. Deutsch (1944-45) also expresses the view that masochism is biologically based, an essential element of femininity, and a condition of erotic pleasure.

Such a theory of masochism has been criticized for lack of empirical support. Horney (1967) argues that the evidence for a biologically based female masochism is insufficient. In her feminist analysis, Elizabeth Waites (1977-78) blames masochism on the "social factors and fixed ideologies concerning the nature of women that are correlated with actual restrictions and with positive rewards for masochistic behavior" (p. 538). It is the combination of social factors and enforced restrictions, not masochism, which is the underlying reason why battered women stay. Waites argues how inadequate the theories of female masochism are for explaining actual behavior. She further discusses the choices of the abused woman and notes the lack of alternatives available to her that would provide a clear escape from pain.

The problems with this intra-individual approach have been well documented elsewhere (Spinetta and Rigler, 1972; Gelles, 1973). This approach lacks confirmation, but does constitute an interesting research approach, which unfortunately has not been subjected to any large-scale investigation. It has been criticized for generalizing from a small group of battered women, often in therapy, to the entire population (Carlson, 1977); for blaming the victim (Flynn, 1977); for endorsing traditional sex role stereotypes; and for failing to take into consideration the environmental factors of leaving (Martin, 1979; Chapman, 1978). The problems of this theoretical approach can be summarized as a combination of inadequate scientific evidence to support the theory and confusion which arises as a result of the inability of the theory to explain adequately which abnormal personality traits are associated with violence.

Frustration-Aggression Theory

The frustration-aggression hypothesis was first specified by Dollard, Doob, Miller, Mowrer, and Seals (1939) and later modified by Miller (1969). The frustration-aggression hypothesis postulates that aggressive behavior results when some goal-directed activity is blocked (frustration). According to Dollard et al. (1939), "the occurrence of aggressive behavior always presupposes the existence of frustration (or the interference with reaching a goal) and always leads to some form of aggression" (p. 1).

This theory assumes that situational factors arouse an aggressive drive which leads, in turn, to aggressive behavior. There is considerable evidence to indicate that situational factors affect the level of spousal violence. The family is a likely setting for aggression because it is the location of many frustrating events. For example, unemployment, job dissatisfaction, and financial difficulties are frequently correlated with incidents of battering (Gelles, 1972; Prescott and Letko, 1977; Roy, 1977). Kathleen Hofeller (1982) indicates that status inequality may also represent a source of frustration.

According to the frustration-aggression hypothesis postulated by Dollard et al. (1939), "aggression may be directed at the object which is perceived as causing the frustration or it may be displaced to some altogether innocent source" (p. 15). In battering situations, a woman is battered either as the cause of the spouse's frustration or as the receiver of his displaced frustration.

Although the frustration-aggression theory seems to be valid, there are some major problems with the theory. The theory would predict that aggression will occur when the victim frustrates the aggressor. This implies that the victim is responsible for the assault. Shainess (1977) suggests that the wife may "trigger" assault by being overly submissive or unexpectedly assertive. If his view is agreed with, then one can "blame the victim" for the assault. Ryan (1976) has analyzed the process of blaming the victim and theorizes that the victim is blamed because such a stance is in the best interest of the non-victimized.

The frustration-aggression hypothesis needs to be modified (Berkowitz, 1962) in that certain situations, aggression may be displaced from the agent responsible for the frustration to a safe object. The target of aggression will be an individual who is unwilling or unable to prevent or retaliate for the battering. This theory has also been criticized for ambiguity in the explanation of why, under similar frustrating circumstances, women are less likely to respond with aggression than men. In general, the frustration-aggression theory fails to explain under what conditions frustration is followed by passive withdrawal (Mead and MacGregor, 1951). Lastly, the frustration-aggression theory fails to address "the crucial problems of how aggressive responses initially begin and the role factors other than interference with an ongoing response sequence (frustration) have in the shaping and maintaining of aggressive behavior" (Bandura, 1973).

Social Learning Theory

Learning theory accounts for violent behavior as a learned social behavior which may be acquired through conditioning or through observational learning and which is maintained by reinforcement of various types (Bandura, 1973; Buss, 1971; Berkowitz, 1969). This theory views violence as a product of a successful learning situation which provides the individual with exposure about the response (violence) and what stimuli are to be followed by the response to cues previously associated with violence. The social learning theory recognizes that the process of learning violence is through exposure to violence and imitation (Bandura et al., 1961). Another aspect of the learning theory looks at how exposure to violence and experience with violence lead to learning norms which approve of violence (Owens and Straus, 1975). A third way to account for this theory is the role model approach, which proposes that violence can be learned by viewing violence in others (Singer, 1971).

The research on the social learning theory is of particular significance in the study of domestic violence. Studies do, in fact, suggest that social learning may indeed be a factor in domestic violence. For example, in some samples approximately 65% of the batterers had been beaten as children and had been exposed to some form of violence in their family (Ganley and Harris, 1979). Martin (1983), Gelles (1975), and Straus, Gelles, and Steinmetz (1980) all commonly report high levels of domestic violence in the batterer's childhood home. Roy (1977) found that 81.1% of the battering husbands came from violent homes, but only one-third of the victims grew up in families in which wife abuse had occurred. Evidence from child abuse research (Steele and Pollock, 1974; Gelles, 1973), together with research on homicidal offenders (Palmer, 1962; Gutmacher, 1960) show that they were recipients of a high level of violence, and much research was devoted to the relevance of explaining violence in the family. However, no definitive conclusions can be drawn regarding why a particular woman is battered. Furthermore, one study shows that there is no relationship between a woman's being abused as a child and her later mistreatment by her husband (Parker and Schumacher, 1977).

Learned Helplessness Theory

The social learning theory has also been used to explain the behavior of the battered women. The theory of learned helplessness in humans is based on Seligman's experimental research with dogs (Seligman and Maier, 1967; Overmier and Seligman, 1967). Seligman administered experiments on the relationship of fear conditioning to instrumental learning. The study showed that prior exposure of dogs to inescapable aversive events results in three basic components: (1) motivational deficits are seen in the experience of uncontrollability; (2) cognitive representation, in which there is the faulty expectation that response or outcome is independent; (3) emotional deficits which interfere with later learning.

Although the battered wife syndrome appears to contain elements of such a description of depression, Walker's (1979) learned helplessness theory has suggested this syndrome as a psychological rationale for explaining why the battered woman becomes a victim, and how the process of victimization is perpetuated to the point of psychological paralysis. Walker suggests that the battered woman may quickly learn that nothing she does changes her husband's behavior. Therefore, the woman eventually accepts that she has no control over her life which results in helplessness, depression, submission, and paralysis.

Studies in the battered women literature do, in fact, commonly report the existence of passivity, depression, or feelings of helplessness in battered women (Dobash and Dobash, 1979; Freeman, 1979; Walker 1979; Ball, 1977). Walker feels that the concept of powerlessness is similar to the concept of helplessness. He further asserts that helplessness is learned on a relative continuum based on an interaction of traditional female role standards and individual personality development. Walker (1977-78) views the battered women as most affected by feelings of helplessness in their relationship with men.

Although the learned helplessness theory seems intuitively valid, there are some problems with the theory. First, in the application of learned helplessness, the definition of learned helplessness closely resembles the symptoms of depression. This suggests that learned helplessness may be a reaction to the naturally occurring depression (Hiroto, 1974). Another problem with this application of Walker's theory is that the theory cannot account for the fact that some women do leave violent spouses without ever having had an opportunity to "practice" necessary behaviors.

Exchange Theory

The major assumption of the exchange theory is that interaction is guided by the pursuit of rewards and the avoidance of punishments. An individual who supplies reward services to another obliges him to fulfill an obligation, and therefore the second individual must furnish benefits to the first (Blau, 1964). According to Goode's interpretation of the exchange theory, women find it difficult to end a relationship which they have come to detest; because they have invested so much and received so little, women are unwilling to leave until the exchanges have been more adequately balanced (Goode, 1973). Applying the conceptual framework of the exchange theory to conjugal violence, couples are bound to each other through an ongoing flow of transactions or exchanges. Violence occurs from those exchanges among family members who are experiencing a continuing residue of resentment because of perceived injustice (Goode, 1973).

However, intrafamilial relations are more complex, and interactions are also maintained by the exchange of other resources besides force alone. Although a couple may receive fewer rewards than they would like, they remain in the interaction because they have few other alternatives to gain rewards from. Homes and Rahe's concept of "distributive justice" explains why. The lack of reciprocity does not automatically mean that family relations will be broken off. According to Homes and Rahe's (1967) study, it is not maximizing rewards minus costs in the absolute which the individual seeks, but "justice" in the distribution of outcomes. Justice prevails when those who invest more in terms of effort, skill, etc., receive more, and those investing less receive less. However, the notion of distributive justice may be violated, as in "when a person's activity does not receive the reward he expected or receives punishment he did not expect, he will be angry, and in anger, the results of aggressive behavior are rewarding" (Homes and Rahe, 1967).

As in the case of other theories, the reason for adoption of a violent response is not explained by the exchange theory. Applying Goode's analysis to the problem of violence in the family, it should be noted that it is easier to explain why a spouse would remain with a violent husband than it is to explain why the husband adopted violence. One may postulate that battered women who stay are heavily socialized into acceptance of the reality and rightness of the family structure. Goode (1974) explains that battered women see no likelihood of altering the terms of exchange and that choice is at best the only real alternative. Conjugal violence may be viewed as the use of violence to inflict "costs" on women. It is noted by exchange theorists that to inflict costs on someone who has injured you is rewarding. Further extension of this view could provide the rationale for wife beating.

According to Scanzoni (1972), marital stability is related to the ratio of costs to rewards as defined individually by the spouses. The motives in deciding whether to remain or leave from the violence may be based on the woman's individual definition attached to the violence or any other costs and on the ratio of these costs to other rewards. Therefore, women are more likely to remain if the reward is greater than the cost. On the other hand, women are more likely to leave if the costs are higher than the rewards. Thus, applying the framework of the exchange theory, one of the major implications of this view is that it only deals with the antecedent conditions of violence rather than how and why violence was adopted to redress a lack of exchange. As a result, the exchange theory needs to be linked with some other theories in order to explain why violence is adopted to redress the injustice and lack of exchange.

Resource Theory

The resource theory was one of the first theories which has been explicitly applied to violence between family members.

According to the perspective which was proposed by Goode (1973), it assumed that all social systems rested to some degree on force or its threat. Force is fundamental to the organization of social systems and is also an inherent aspect of family interaction. Goode further argues that the greater the resources a person can command, the less he will actually deploy or use force in an overt manner (Goode, 1974: 628).

Allen and Straus' (1980) application of this theory addresses the same perspective of the greater the absolute number of resources at the husband's disposal, the less the likelihood that he will resort to using the resource of violence. Recently, violence began to be added to the traditional list of resources (e.g., income, education). Violence is commonly used as a resource, especially when other resources are insufficient or lacking. For example, a husband who wants to be the dominant figure in his family but has a poor education and a job which is low in prestige and income may have to resort to violence in order to maintain a dominant position. This perspective is supported by a study (O'Brien, 1971) which concludes that there is a greater tendency to use force and violence on family members in families when the husband's achieved status was lower than his wife's compared to families in which the husband had the higher prestige job.

The resource theory is also the basis behind the claim that the greater the number of resources which the woman has, the less likely that she will remain in abusive situations. According to a study by Nielsen et al. (1979), economic conditions--the woman's employment, job options, earning capacity, and number of children--are paramount in a woman's decision to remain with the batterer. The battered woman's fear of leaving and provoking her husband's revenge is another view of violence as a resource upon which a husband can maintain his marriage. Although the resource theory appears to be a valid view of violence, the function of resources in family violence in the middle and upper classes also needs to be further studied in order not to limit the application of this theory to any specific group of individuals or families.

In conclusion, the preceding theories attempt to explain the determinants of physical violence within the family. These theories contribute some helpful insights into the understanding of the problem of conjugal violence. Since each theory falls short in some aspect, it is necessary to build upon existing theories of wife abuse to extend theoretical perspectives of culture-of-violence. These theories should be evaluated by their usefulness for understanding Korean women and their practice applications.

CHAPTER 5

The Study

Although the wife abuse phenomenon has a long history, it is only recently that people have begun to study the problem more seriously. Therefore, the amount of empirical study available is relatively limited. Particularly, examination and review of the available literature revealed that very little research has been conducted on the Korean battered woman. The present study is designed and implemented with the expectation of achieving specific contributions in meeting the urgent unmet needs of battered women. Otherwise, these Korean immigrant battered women will continue to be isolated, and their problems with battering will increase.

The purpose of the present study was to investigate selected socio-cultural dimensions involved with the battering of Korean immigrant women living in the United States. Based upon the material discussed in the previous chapters, it is possible to construct a schematic model relating each of the key variables of this study in a causal fashion. Such a model (Thoennes, 1981) is presented in Figure 2 on the following page.

The Conceptual Model outlined in Figure 2 constitutes an exploratory study. The relationship between cultural factors and wife abuse has been explored empirically. The following major questions were offered, based on the study objectives and the model.

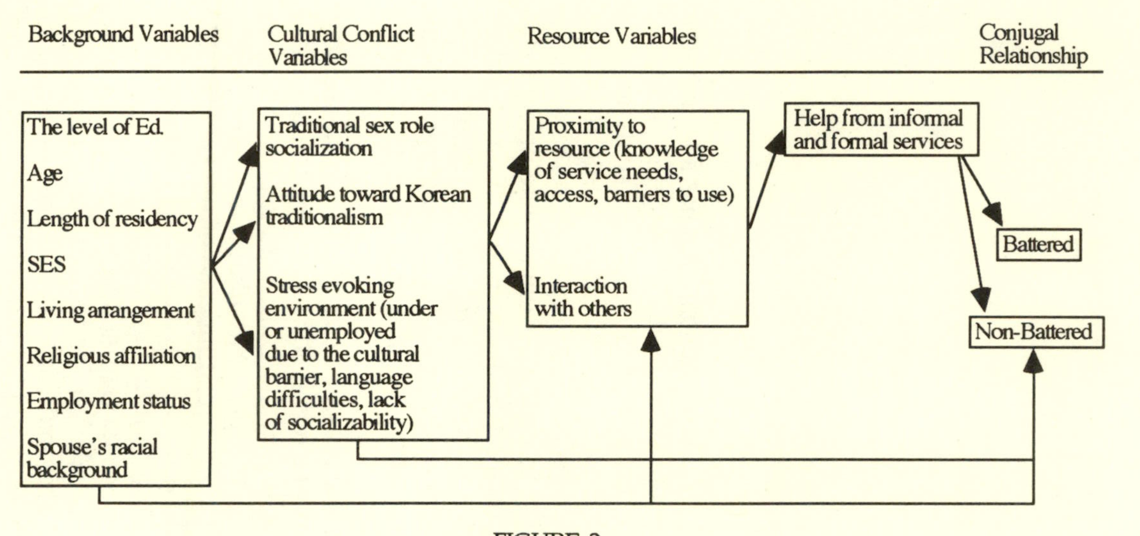

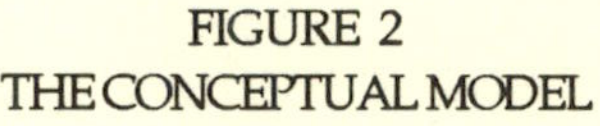

FIGURE 2
THE CONCEPTUAL MODEL

1. Is there a significant relationship between the level of abuse and the demographic variables? (the level of education, age, marital status, length of residency, socio-economic status, religious affiliation, and living arrangements).

2. What are the characteristics of the wife abuse experienced by the study ?

3. Is there a significant relationship between women's attitudes toward Korean traditionalism and wife abuse?

4. Is there a significant relationship between the rigid sex role performances and wife abuse?

5. Is there a significant relationship between stress-evoking factors and wife abuse?

6. Is there a significant difference in the level of abuse occurring in two-career families and traditional families?

7. Is there a significant difference in the level of abuse occurring in Korean-Korean couples and Korean-American couples?

8. Is there a significant relationship between wife abuse and stress-related symptoms experienced by Korean women?

9. What sources are most frequently utilized by the Korean battered women? (knowledge of service needs, utilization patterns, access barriers to the use of formal services).

The following six hypotheses related to the outcome of wife abuse were developed:

1. The level of wife abuse is directly related to the demographic background of the subject.

2. The more traditional Korean immigrant women are, the more likely they are to experience wife abuse.

3. The more rigid sex roles Korean immigrant couples perform, the more likely they are to experience wife abuse.

4. The more stress-evoking factors Korean immigrant women face, the more likely they are to experience wife abuse.

5. The level of wife abuse is directly related to the employment status of women.

6. The level of wife abuse is directly related to the stress-related symptoms.

The term battered women used in the study refers to adult women who have been intentionally or involuntarily physically abused in ways that caused the risk of pain or injury, or who have been the victims of threats of violence (e.g., threatened with a knife) by men with whom they have established cohabitating relationships, whether or not within a legally married state. The term "battered" does not include verbal abuse unless it occurs in conjunction with the risk of physical force. Although these are undeniably damaging and painful, the overall consensus among samples of the present study have not perceived the verbal abuse as an actual account of wife abuse. Within the confines of this study, the terms "wife abuse," "spouse abuse," "woman abuse," "family abuse," "conjugal violence," and "domestic violence" were used interchangeably and will refer to a woman being physically beaten.

For the purpose of the present study, a woman was defined as "battered" if she marked any item beyond the first two items on the Current Abuse Checklist. Furthermore, in order to be classified as a battered woman, the woman must have gone through the incident of abuse at least twice in the past two years. After the woman found herself in an abusive relationship with a man once, and she remained in the situation even if it occurred more than a second time, she is defined as a battered woman.

Korean women in this study include those aged 18 years and older, residing in the United States less than 10 years, who share the Korean language and culture, and whose ancestors originated in Korea. The term "Korean women" is interchangeable with "Korean immigrant women" in this study.

The term "Korean Traditionalism" refers to the attitude that the established patterns of the past in Korea are the best guidance in deciding the behavior in the present. This attitude opposes change away from past cultural values and norms and justifies its actions and values on the basis of the presumed accumulated wisdom inherent in past forms (Theodorson and Theodorson, 1969). For the purpose of the present study, this was operationally defined as the scores obtained on the Korean Traditionalism Scale.

Within the confines of the present study, the term "stress-evoking environment" refers to situations which precipitate high demand, high constraints, and can be considered a source of frustration. It refers to a conflictive situation within an individual (or a family) due to the differences between Korean and American cultures, both of which provide certain acceptance and contradiction. Furthermore, these situations affect the individual's adequacy in performing socio-cultural roles and even facilitate the interference with daily living. Specific variables employed in this study are: status inconsistency, language difficulty, and lack of sociability.

The term "rigid sex role" refers to social norms which determine the appropriateness of specific behaviors for the two sexes. In every society, specific behavioral expectations and standards are applied to men and women; deviations are generally subject to negative sanctions. Rigid sex roles can be viewed as the product of the process of socialization and generally unconsciously internalized, and they come to be taken for granted culturally. As a function of this division of labor, D'Andrade (1966), suggests that the sex roles can be traced back to a learning process in which an increasing range of activities are standardized as typical of a particular sex, without reference to biological differences. For the purpose of the present study, this was operationally defined as the results obtained on the items on the sex role performance in individual households.

"Stress-related symptoms" refer to a number of psychological and physical disorders experienced by the individuals in this study. This will be operationally defined in this study as the scores obtained on the Twenty-Two Items Screening Score (Appendix Part V), which contained items indicating whether the subject experienced various physical and psychological symptoms after the abusive relationship.

The term "level of abuse" refers to frequency and severity of abuse which will be operationally defined in this study as the scores obtained on items comprising two indices: type and frequency of abusive acts and the types of injuries.

The sample chosen for this study included 150 Korean immigrant women. The participants consisted of married and unmarried women, aged 21 years old and over, who have resided not more than 10 years in Chicago, Illinois. The sample was chosen through a purposeful snowballing method. This specific method was chosen as opposed to random sampling, because it is not very feasible for this study, nor is there any comprehensive and up-to-date directory of Korean women immigrants in the area.

There are obviously basic difficulties in attempting to do survey research on a population which is resident in scattered locations. Because of the researcher's familiarity with the Korean community, as well as their availability for study, some participants purposefully selected for the study group were interracially married Korean women. Approaches were undertaken to Korean women individually and in groups, explaining the purposes of the study and ascertaining their willingness to respond to the interview. The list of sources are: (a) Korean Community Services, (b) Korean Christian Churches, (c) Korean Women Alumni Association, (d) Korean Travel Agencies, (e) a Korean Buddhist Temple, (f) Korean Association in Chicago, (g) the Korean language daily newspaper in Chicago, (h) Korean-American Spouses Association of Wives, (i) Korean grocery stores, (j) Korean restaurants, (k) Korean clothing stores, (l) Korean shoe repair shops, (m) Korean wig shops, (n) Korean herb shops, (o) Korean book and record shops, (p) a Korean fortune teller's house, (q) Korean hair salons, (r) Korean internist offices, and (s) Korean nursery schools.

A total of 199 Korean women residing in Chicago were approached to be interviewed: 12 could not be reached due to incorrect addresses; 16 could not be reached due to incorrect telephone numbers; in 21 cases, the interview was never completed. As a result, a final total sample of 150 was included in the data analysis of this study.

Data was collected by means of a questionnaire or structured interviews of respondents by the investigator. Telephone numbers were obtained from the directory of Korean associations and lists of subscribers of Korean newspapers. Some Korean women were contacted by telephone for face-to-face interviews; some were approached by the investigator individually or in groups, depending on how accessible they were. For example, a group of questionnaires was distributed after the introductory explanation. To ensure confidentiality, a separate desk in the corner of the room was prepared for the collection of the returned questionnaires with envelopes. In addition, considering the nature of the study, interviews were conducted without the husband's presence.

During the first phase of data collection, initial contacts were made with referral sources, such as Korean travel agencies, Korean churches, temples, etc. After the introductory letters were mailed out, visitations and meetings with representatives from each place were made in order to facilitate their cooperation for the study.

During the second phase, structured interviews were administered by the researcher at various designated locations, including churches, temples, restaurants, shops, nursery schools, fortune tellers, etc. During the final phase, home visit interviews were administered after telephone contacts with women from the directory of Korean associations and the lists of subscribers of Korean newspapers. This approach was purposefully used in order to include women who stay at home most of the time. Toward the ending part of the final phase, the researcher collected data from interracially married Korean women through their friend network channel.

Difficulties in obtaining a study population with regard to Korean immigrants were reported by many researchers (Hurh, Kim, and Kim, 1979; Choy, 1979; Yu, 1983). As the researcher has lived and worked with the people in this particular study group, the foreknowledge of the sample led to guidelines for selecting samples, and conducting interviews. In addition, the researcher's ability to speak the Korean language facilitated a personal approach to interviewing.

There are at least six limitations of the design of this study which must be considered in evaluating results.

1. All of the Korean women who participated were volunteers who must must have felt somewhat uncomfortable about talking of personal, often painful, experiences. The cultural reluctance among Korean women is another aspect which needs to be considered. Their reluctance to express their problems openly is probably due to an overwhelming concern that they may be viewed as a problem to the community. There is also the probability that respondents who were willing to participate in the study may have had fewer problems than others.

2. It should be evident that a snowballing technique provided a biased sample that would not be a representative sample of all Korean immigrant women in the United States. Although every effort was taken to minimize the potential bias on the selection of the sample, the final sample turned out to be probably more outgoing Korean immigrant women rather than home-bound Korean women.

3. Data was solely dependent upon the memory of Korean women, and data was retrospective in nature. One might further suppose that certain errors of memory would have occurred. In addition, all information about the spouse was second-hand data. Therefore, it is possible that a woman's feelings of vulnerability or simply the tendency to block out memories of their experiences with violence could have influenced data on the accounts of abuse and the spouse's behavior.

4. In most research with non-Western subjects, an immediate obstacle to overcome was the language barrier. All respondents in this study had difficulty with the English language. Difficulties involved in translation

are well-known (Hurh and Kim, 1988), although care was taken to ensure the best possible equivalent word. As other Korean researchers indicated (Koh and Koh, 1974), many English terms are often not translatable or are very difficult to translate into Korean language without elaboration. One must also pay a great deal of attention to honorifics when translating from English into Korean.

5. This study is also limited by the construction and the limited administration of the instruments used. Some instruments used in this study were designed specifically for use in this study, and thus do not have a history of use in research. Since no prior studies of Korean battered women were available, it is not possible to compare the findings of this study with any appropriate previous study on Korean women. The processing of the data collectively was emphasized to ensure a reasonable level of confidence in the study findings. Furthermore, the data analysis needs to be extended to multivariate analysis to identify some of the most important study variables affecting wife abuse among all the significant variables.

6. Due to the aforementioned bias in the sampling design, it is difficult to assert broad applications of study findings to the larger body of Korean women in the United States. Therefore the generalization of the findings is limited to the Korean women in Chicago, Illinois.

While saying that she will leave her abusive husband,
she gives birth to three children.

Korean Proverb

CHAPTER 6

Findings

This chapter presents the findings of the data collected on the respondents' demographic characteristics and analyzes the characteristics of the wife abuse on selected variables, followed by the presentation of the measured respondents' existing stress related symptoms and the identification of sources of help in meeting the needs of the Korean women respondents.

Demographic Characteristics

An overview of the major demographic data of one hundred and fifty participants residing in Chicago, Illinois, is presented in Table 3. The age distribution of the respondents ranged from twenty-one to sixty-one years.

The median age was 36 and the mean age was 36.2. The majority of the women (75%) had completed high school, and 27.3% of them were college graduates. On the other hand, 4.7% of the respondents had no education or less than a complete elementary education.

Although most of the women (82%) were currently married, 17% were divorced or were living together without legal marriage. The respondents' length of residence in the United States ranged from one year to ten years. Nearly one-half of the respondents were newcomers who had lived in America five years or less. The average length of residence

TABLE 3

DEMOGRAPHIC CHARACTERISTICS OF RESPONDENTS

Demographic Characteristics	Number	Percent	Cumulated Percent
Total	150	100.00	100.0
Age			
21 - 24	7	4.6	4.6
25 - 29	28	18.7	23.3
30 - 39	69	46.0	69.3
40 - 49	36	24.0	93.3
50 - 59	8	6.0	99.3
60 and over	1	0.7	100.0
Educational Level			
None - less than 6th grade	7	4.7	4.7
Completed elementary school	12	8.0	12.7
Completed 9th grade	18	12.0	24.7
Completed high school	45	30.0	54.7
Completed two years of college	27	18.0	72.7
Completed four years of college	35	23.3	96.0
Completed graduate school	6	4.0	100.0
Marital Status			
Never married	2	1.3	1.3
Married	123	82.0	83.3
Separated	8	5.3	88.7
Divorced	10	6.7	95.3
Widowed	1	0.7	96.0
Living together	6	4.0	100.0
Length of Residence in the U.S.			
1 year	17	11.3	11.3
2 years	5	3.4	4.7
3 years	16	10.6	25.4
4 years	17	11.4	36.6
5 years	16	10.6	47.4
6 years	9	6.0	53.3
7 years	11	7.4	60.6
8 years	15	10.0	70.6

TABLE 3 (continued)

9 years	13	8.6	79.6
10 years	31	20.6	100.0
Monthly Family Income			
Less than $500	7	4.7	4.7
$ 500 - $ 999	16	10.6	15.3
$1,000 - $1,499	26	17.4	32.7
$1,500 - $1,999	20	13.3	46.0
$2,000 - $2,499	30	20.0	66.0
$2,500 - $2,999	13	8.6	74.6
$3,000 - $3,999	17	11.4	86.0
$4,000 or more	21	14.0	100.0
Employment Status			
Unemployed	47	30.4	30.4
Employed	103	69.6	100.0
Religion			
Buddhism	20	18.0	18.0
Protestant	80	53.3	71.3
Catholic	15	10.0	81.3
Confucianism	0	0.0	81.3
No religion	26	17.3	98.6
Other (describe)	2	1.3	100.0
Living Arrangements			
Dwelling Place			
Single residential household	76	50.7	50.7
Rented apartment	68	45.3	96.8
Relatives' home	2	1.3	97.3
Friends' home	4	2.7	100.0
Household			
Living alone	4	2.7	
with spouse	128	85.3	
with children	108	72.0	
with relatives	5	3.4	
with grandchildren	3	2.0	
with friends	2	1.3	
with in-laws	14	9.3	

among the respondents was five years. Approximately 70% were employed and their family income ranged from $500 to $4000 per month.

The majority (74%) of the women reported religious beliefs, and more than half of the respondents (53%) were affiliated with the Protestant faith, while 18% were Buddhist and 10% were Catholics.

Of the 150 women, about one-half (51%) of them lived in single residential households (27% owned homes; 24% rented homes), while 45% lived in apartments. A little over 72% had at least one child or more living at home; 53% had two children; and 19% had more than three. A little less than 10% lived in households with their parents-in-law, and 4% lived alone.

Characteristics of the Abuse

Level of abuse

The type of abuse acts and the injuries resulting from the abuse are presented in Table 4. Out of a total of 150 respondents, 60% of the women (N=90) reported the experience of abuse while 40% (N=60) were found to be nonbattered women. There was a wide range in the abusive acts and injuries. Of the 90 battered cases, 57% of the women indicated they were hit with a closed fist, and in 42% of the cases, men slapped the women. 24% of the women were choked by their spouses. 20% of the battered women reported that their spouses had threatened them with a knife or gun. In two cases, the man did actually attempt to kill his wife. 24% of the women reported that they were abused by their spouse at least once a week, while another 37% suffered from wife abuse at least once a month.

As a result of abuse, 70% of the women said that they had bruises. In 38% of the cases, women reported black eyes, while

TABLE 4
LEVEL OF ABUSE

Degree	Description	Percent of Battered Cases (N=90)	N
Abusive acts:			
0	My husband/partner yelled at me	-	125
0	My husband/partner swore at me	78.9	71
1	My husband/partner destroyed my property	43.3	39
1	My husband/partner threw an object at me	51.1	46
Moderate			
1	My husband/partner threatened to hit me with an object	34.4	31
1	My husband/partner threatened to hit with his fist	56.7	51
2	My husband/partner hit me with a closed fist	56.7	51
Rather Severe			
2	My husband/partner slapped me	42.2	38
2	My husband/partner hit me with an object	21.1	19
3	My husband/partner threatened me with a knife	15.6	14
3	My husband/partner threatened to kill me	22.2	20
Moderately Severe			
3	My husband/partner threatened to kill himself	14.4	13
3	My husband/partner threatened me with a gun	4.4	4
4	My husband/partner forced me to have sex with him	36.7	33
Severe			
4	My husband/partner squeezed or pinched me	25.6	23
4	My husband/partner choked me	24.4	22
4	My husband/partner burned me	4.4	4
4	My husband/partner broke a bone	7.8	7
4	My husband/partner stabbed me	3.3	3
Very Severe			
5	My husband/partner attempted to kill me	2.2	2

TABLE 4 (continued)

Resultant injuries:		
Moderate		
1 Bruises	70.0	63
1 Black eye	37.8	34
1 Minor cuts or burns	30.0	27
2 Cuts, burns, or bruises requiring medical attention	14.4	13
Rather Severe		
2 Concussion	16.7	15
2 Damage to teeth	10.0	9
Moderately Severe		
3 Broken bones	8.9	8
3 Joint injury	3.3	3
3 Spinal injury	1.1	1
4 Injury to internal organs	2.2	2
Severe		
4 Miscarriage	8.9	8
4 Emotional/mental distress requiring medical care	28.9	26
5 Physical injury requiring hospitalization	6.7	6

Frequency of abuse:

At least once/day	3.3%
At least once/week	24.1%
At least once/month	37.3%
At least once/year	38.3%

another 30% said that they had minor cuts or burns. 17% of the battered women indicated they had concussions and another 19% said they had broken bones or teeth. Nine percent of the women experienced miscarriages while another 29% experienced emotional/mental distress requiring medical care. Seven percent of the women were hospitalized due to the physical injury from wife abuse.

Because the level of abuse cannot be measured by either the abusive acts or the injuries alone, a combination of both the abusive acts and the resultant injuries has been used to observe the level of abuse for the present study. In order to obtain an overall measure of abuse, cases were assigned a score of one for "high" and a zero for "low" on each of the five dimensions of abusive acts.

The severity of injuries was also given ratings; the higher the score, the more severe the injuries were thought to be. These scores were then summed. For example, a score of three indicates that the spouse used his fists to cause bruises, but not broken bones. The results are presented in Tables 4 and 5. In only seven cases was the abuse scored as one.

Opening argument immediately before the abuse

47% of the battered women argued on problems about in-laws and relatives immediately before the incidence of abuse, and 44% of the women had an argument about children. 34% of the battered argued on problems about money, and 32% argued about employment. 27% of the women reported arguments about problems related to their husbands' drinking when abuse occurred, while 42% of the women said that they had argued about chores and responsibilities (see Table 6).

Wives' response to abuse

58% of the battered women said they verbally fought back the abuser. 33% of the battered women said that they cried and begged the abuser to stop. 29% of the battered women reported that they fought back physically during the battering incident. Only 3% said they went to stay elsewhere, another 3% of the battered women actually called the police, 21% merely stared at the abuser, and 9% tried to ignore the abuse (See Table 7).

Behavior after abusive incident

91% of the battered women reported crying after an abusive incident, and 47% of the battered women apologized to their husbands after the abuse took place. 32% of the battered women went to sleep while another 20% thought about revenge for a period following an abuse incident (see Table 8).

It was also interesting to note the perceptions the women had of the abuses which were taking place. Fourteen battered women (16%) who had abuse incidents in their relationship still felt they were not being abused. Of the remaining women (N=76), self-defined as battered women, 23 (26%) reported the first abuse took place in Korea, and 53 (59%) reported that the first abusive incident occurred after immigration to the United States.

The great majority (92% of the total 150 women) in the present study answered "yes" to the question asking if they know any Korean, including themselves, who has been battered by her husband. It would appear that wife abuse is not an unfamiliar topic to the study respondents and also indicates that the knowledge of wife abuse in the Korean community is high.

TABLE 5

TOTAL INTERCORRELATION MATRIX FOR ABUSE (Pearson correlation coefficients)

Variable	Abusive Acts	Injury	Level of Abuse (Acts & Injuries)
Abusive acts		.870 ($p < .05$)	.954 ($p < .05$)
Injury			.937 ($p < .05$)
Level of abuse			

N = 150

TABLE 6

OPENING ARGUMENT IMMEDIATELY BEFORE THE ABUSE

Arguments About	Percent of Battered Cases (N=90)	N
Children	44.4	40
Money	34.4	31
Sex	17.7	16
Religion	16.7	15
Outside activity	20.0	18
Drinking	26.7	24
Other women	11.1	10
In-laws and relatives	46.7	42
Chores and responsibilities	42.2	38
Food, cooking	20.0	18
Other men	2.2	2
Employment	32.2	29
Friends and associates	17.8	16

Demographic Characteristics of Battered Korean Women

This information is based on the ninety cases who had battering relationships. These results are reported for the woman's current and past battering status, as reported at the time of the interview. The battered wives ranged in age from twenty-one to fifty-six. Due to the nature of this study and general characteristics of overall Korean immigrants, the majority of the battered women (N= 69) were married.

An examination of the education levels among the battered women reveals that 40% of the battered women had completed high school, 13% had completed a four-year college, and two percent had graduate degrees. Relative to the nonbattered women (5%), nearly 10% of the battered women had less than elementary education or no formal education. The battered women also differed from the nonbattered women in religious affiliation. About two times as many battered women are attending churches as compared to nonbattered women. Furthermore, many battered women stated they were told by a minister they should be good Christians and forgive their husbands unconditionally.

The battered women differed significantly from the nonbattered women in length of residence in the United States ($x^2 = 30.12$, $p < .05$), and ($F = 4.25$, $p < .05$). About three times as many women experienced battering during three to five years residence in the United States as compared to the nonbattered women. This data supports what seems to be the general experience of Korean immigrants: they are confronting the harsh realities of adjusting to a new environment after the cultural shock of immigration.

In the area of income, there are no significant differences between battered women and nonbattered women. The living arrangements of battered and nonbattered women are

TABLE 7

WIVES' RESPONSE TO ABUSE

Description of Response	Percent of Battered Cases (N=90)	N
Fight back physically	28.9	26
Fight back verbally	57.8	52
Order him to stop	8.9	8
Stare at him	21.1	19
Scream for help	17.8	16
Cry, beg him to stop	33.3	30
Try to protect self	77.8	7
Try to leave the scene	15.6	14
Go stay elsewhere	3.3	3
Call the police	3.3	3
Try to ignore it–do nothing	8.9	8

TABLE 8

BEHAVIOR AFTER ABUSIVE INCIDENT

Behavior	Percent of Battered Cases (N=90)	N
Cry	91.1	82
Apologize	46.7	42
Eat	8.9	8
Drink	10.0	9
Use drugs	4.0	10
Watch television	6.7	6
Leave the house	13.3	12
Go to sleep	32.2	29
Make love	14.4	13
Think about revenge	20.0	18

distributed across the range of possibilities. 47% of battering incidents occurred in single residential housing, while another 45 of the battered women (50%) are living in apartments. For the battered and nonbattered group, those differences were similar to the living arrangements that would be expected between the two groups. However, there were significant differences ($x^2 = 17.19$, $p < .05$) when comparing the battered women and nonbattered women living with children or in-laws.

In comparing demographic characteristics of battered and nonbattered women, there were similarities in much of the background data. The hypothesis that the level of wife abuse is directly related to the demographic background of the subject was partially supported in the length of residence in the United States, and the living arrangements with children and in-laws. No significant statistical differences in age, educational level, religious affiliation, and income were found between the two compared groups. This is an indication that demographical background does not necessarily provide a prediction of wife abuse in Korean immigrant families. It is fair to say that almost any woman could be abused; however, most battered Korean women share certain demographic characteristics which increase the likelihood of their becoming battered women.

Relationships of Cultural Conflict to Wife Abuse

In this study, the cultural conflict was viewed by different variables which were divided into three components: attitude toward Korean traditionalism, sex-role performance, and the stress-evoking environments. These variables were used to measure the relationship between cultural conflict and wife abuse.

Women's attitudes towards Korean traditionalism

Items on the Traditional Attitude Questionnaire were used to obtain a measure of traditional attitudes toward marital interaction, dating and marriage, childrearing, and old Korean beliefs. In order to obtain an overall measure of the attitude toward Korean traditionalism, cases were assigned a score of one for "most traditional" and a zero for "least traditional" on each level of attitude (i.e., always = 4; often = 3; sometimes = 2; hardly ever = 1). Scores between 38 and 60 were rated as "high" in traditionalism, and scores between 15 and 37 were rated as "low."

Of the study respondents, 47 (52%) of the battered women and only 19 (31%) of the nonbattered women were rated "high" on attitude toward traditionalism (see Tables 9, 10, 11). The difference between battered and nonbattered groups was statistically significant ($x^2 = 6.17$, $p < .05$, $F = 7.91$, $p < .05$).

The respondents in the battered group who scored higher in the direction of level of abuse in the Abuse scale, also scored high in the direction of Attitude toward Korean Traditionalism. At the same time, the women in the nonbattered group who scored lower in the Abuse Scale, also scored in the direction of having a less traditional attitude on the measurement of attitude toward Korean traditionalism.

There is a linear relationship between the level of abuse and the attitude toward Korean traditionalism ($p < .05$). Results from the above analysis do confirm the hypothesis that the more traditional Korean immigrant women are, the more likely they are to experience wife abuse.

TABLE 9

ANALYSIS OF VARIANCE OF LEVEL OF ABUSE BY RESPONDENTS' ATTITUDE TOWARD TRADITIONALISM

Source	df	SS	ms	F	P-value
Traditionalism	1	1,189.7772	1,189.772	7.91	Is Significant ($p < .05$)
Error	148	21,955.49203	150.380		
Total	149	23,145.2702			

TABLE 10

RESPONDENTS' DISTRIBUTION ON ATTITUDE TOWARD TRADITIONALISM BY BATTERED AND NONBATTERED KOREAN WOMEN

Attitude Toward Korean Traditionalism	Nonbattered Women No. (%)	Battered Women No. (%)	Total No. (%)
High (more traditional)	19 (12.7)	47 (31.3)	66 (44.0)
Low (less traditional)	41 (27.3)	43 (28.7)	84 (56.0)
Total	60 (40.0)	90 (60.0)	150 (100.0)

$x^2 = 6.17$, $p < .05$

TABLE 11

CORRELATION MATRIX: RESPONDENTS' ATTITUDE TOWARD KOREAN TRADITIONALISM AND WIFE ABUSE

Abusive Acts	Resultant Injuries	Level of Wife Abuse (Acts & Injuries)	Attitudes Toward Traditionalism
Resultant Injuries			
Level of Wife Abuse (Acts & Injuries)	.937 .0001		
Attitude Toward Traditionalism	.255 .002	.226 .005	

N = 150

Rigid sex role performance

A measure of the sex role performance was obtained by the response to the question of how the couple divided household tasks in their home. For the response, thirteen different household tasks were given from cooking to making decisions to purchasing housing.

The respondents were then asked to check their role in the home in terms of their relative performance of each of these items. Category A refers to the rigid sex role expected by the wife alone, Category B refers to the role expected to be performed by both the husband and the wife, and Category C refers to the husband performing a role alone (see Table 12).

From viewing the table, it was observed that in most of the respondents' families from battered and nonbattered groups, the wives predominantly performed most of the household task items. In the remaining three task items--paying bills and making decisions to buy something (television, furniture, house, etc.)--Korean husbands were substantially involved. The reasons for these results were due to the management of the family budget, which requires bookkeeping, planning of family and other financial decisions, which is compatible with the husband's role as the main breadwinner in the family (Hurh and Kim, 1984). An exception to these patterns of clear division of sex role performance is found from the observation of nonbattered families in which wives share some tasks with their spouses. However, even in this situation, the husband's sharing in the nonbattered home is very limited to his rigid traditional sex role in the family.

This is another indication of the persistence of the rigid traditional division of sex role performance in the battered Korean families. This observation leads us to the question of why the rigid sex role persists so pervasively in the Korean battered immigrant families. Obviously, as Hurh and Kim (1984) indicated, the past traditional socialization of the respondents may

TABLE 12

DISTRIBUTION OF RESPONDENTS' SEX ROLE PERFORMANCE IN THE HOUSEHOLD TASKS BY BATTERED AND NONBATTERED WOMEN AND SPOUSE

		Battered			Nonbattered			Totals	
		Wife	Husband	Both	Wife	Husband	Both		
Category	Task	No. (%)	No. (%)	No. (%)	No. (%)	No. (%)	No. (%)	No.	(%)
A	Cooking	77 (51.3)		13 (8.6)	48 (32.0)		12 (8.0)	150	100.0
A	Washing dishes	69 (46.0)	2 (1.3)	19 (12.7)	40 (26.7)	2 (1.3)	18 (12.0)	150	100.0
A	Laundry	66 (44.0)	4 (2.6)	20 (13.3)	35 (23.3)	4 (2.6)	21 (14.0)	150	100.0
A	Driving the car	13 (8.6)	42 (28.0)	34 (22.7)	5 (3.3)	14 (9.3)	41 (27.3)	150	100.0
A	Shopping for groceries	43 (28.7)	2 (1.3)	45 (30.0)	20 (13.3)		40 (26.7)	150	100.0
A	Buying clothes	55 (36.7)	2 (1.3)	33 (22.0)	30 (20.0)	3 (2.0)	27 (18.0)	150	100.0
C	Paying bills	39 (26.0)	32 (21.3)	19 (12.7)	16 (10.6)	20 (13.0)	24 (16.0)	150	100.0

A	Taking care of children	61 (40.7)	1 (0.6)	28 (18.7)	27 (18.0)	0 (0.0)	33 (22.0)	150	100.0
B	Talking to teacher about children	56 (37.3)	13 (8.7)	21 (14.0)	12 (8.0)	5 (3.3)	43 (28.7)	150	100.0
A	Making bed	67 (44.6)	1 (0.6)	22 (14.6)	27 (18.0)	4 (2.6)	29 (19.3)	150	100.0
B	Cleaning the house	68 (45.3)	1 (0.6)	21 (14.0)	23 (15.3)	4 (2.6)	33 (22.0)	150	100.0
B	Making a decision to buy something	18 (12.0)	30 (20.0)	42 (28.0)	7 (4.6)	5 (3.3)	48 (32.0)	150	100.0
B	Making a decision to buy a house	10 (8.0)	43 (28.7)	37 (24.7)	5 (3.3)	4 (2.6)	51 (34.0)	150	100.0

be a major factor. This is supported by the fact that a much larger majority of both battered husbands and wives adhere to rigid sex role patterns compared to the performance of sex roles by nonbattered families.

As shown in Tables 13 and 14, about 58% of the battered families, which is 35% of total respondents, shows high congruency to the rigid sex role performance in their houses. On the other hand, only 17% of the nonbattered families perform the rigid sex role in dividing household tasks. Interestingly, 23% of the nonbattering families (57% of nonbattered cases), share the same sex role while there is 16% sharing in the battering home (28% of the battered cases). The result from the data supported the significant differences of performing sex roles between the two groups ($x^2 = 25.14$, $p < .05$, $F = 18.49$, $p < .05$). Thus, the rigid sex role performance is clearly seen as associated with wife abuse. It is substantiated that battered couples are more rigidly interacting into the female and male sex role stereotype. The hypothesis that the more rigid the sex roles Korean immigrant couples perform, the more likely they are to experience wife abuse was substantiated.

Stress-evoking factors

A measure of the stress-evoking factors was obtained through the variables which are the indicators of conflicting situations within an individual due to the differences between Korean and American cultures. Situations which can be considered as a source of frustration are status inconsistency, language difficulty, and lack of sociability.

1. Status Inconsistency: In the battered women, the current employment level for women tended to be lower than the employment level in Korea. The study actually shows seventy-two battered women came from higher employment levels than their current low level of employment. Where they were once either semi- professionals or held clerical positions in Korea,

TABLE 13

CONGRUENCY OF THE RIGID SEX ROLE IN BATTERED AND NONBATTERED WOMEN

	Battered Women No. (%)	Nonbattered Women No. (%)	Total No. (%)
High congruency to rigid sex role	47 (31.3)	19 (12.7)	66 (44.0)
Sharing sex role	25 (16.7)	34 (22.7)	59 (39.3)
Low congruency to rigid sex role	13 (8.7)	16 (10.7)	29 (19.3)
Total	90 (60.0)	60 (40.0)	150 (100.0)

TABLE 14

ANALYSIS OF VARIANCE OF LEVEL OF ABUSE BY RESPONDENTS' CONGRUENCY TO THE RIGID SEX ROLE

Source	df	SS	m	F	P-value
Rigid Sex Role p<.05	2	2,714.9536	2,714.9536	18.49	significant
Error	147	16,442.0726	146.8042		
Total	149	19,157.0263			

they now hold manual level positions in the United States. By contrast, only thirty-eight nonbattered women came from higher employment levels to current lowered employment levels.

In the battering group, the current employment level for men also tended to be lower than that for pre-immigration employment status in Korea. Of the total 150 cases, 35% of men from the battering group (58% of the 90 battering cases) are experiencing status inconsistency in their current employment level when compared to their pre-immigration status. In contrast, only seven percent of the men from the nonbattering group (18% of 60 nonbattering cases) came from a higher employment level to a current lower level (see Table 15). This result also shows significant differences between the two groups ($x^2 = 25.2$, $p < .05$). Thus, the hypothesis that the more stress-evoking factors Korean immigrant women face, the more likely they are to experience wife abuse was fully substantiated with regard to status inconsistency.

2. Language Difficulty: About 90% of battered women reported that they have problems in speaking English. About one-fifth of the battered women indicated their English abilities are "poor" or "not at all." By contrast, no one from the nonbattering group reported that they cannot speak English at all. One of the most important variables affecting cultural adjustments is language as indicated by Hurh and Kim (1984). This is true for the respondents in this study in relation to the battering. The results show significant differences between battered and nonbattered women with regard to wife abuse ($x^2 = 8.49$, $p < .05$). With such a limited ability in English, the majority of Korean women must be experiencing a great deal of frustration and stress in daily lives. The hypothesis that the more stress-evoking factors Korean immigrant women face, the more likely they are to experience wife abuse was partially substantiated with regard to language difficulty.

3. Lack of Sociability: A measure for lack of sociability was obtained through the variables of frequency of going out, talking to friends or relatives, mobility (driving a car), and participation in clubs and organizations. Social isolation due to the lack of sociability has been written about in the literature as occurring both as part of and as a result of the wife abuse (Walker, 1979; Martin, 1979). Twenty nonbattered women go out every day. In contrast, seven women from the battering group hardly ever go outside their home. Data analysis shows the significant difference between these two groups ($x^2 = 12.51$, $p < .05$).

At the same time of the total 150 cases (36%), 55 of the nonbattered women were talking to their friends or relatives at least once a week while close to half of the battered women were talking to their friends or relatives from less than once a week to hardly ever. In terms of access to mobility and the ability to drive a car, there is no significant difference between battered

TABLE 15

STATUS INCONSISTENCY IN THE EMPLOYMENT STATUS OF KOREAN MEN WITH BATTERED AND NONBATTERED WOMEN

	Men from Battering Group No. (%)	Men from Nonbattering Group No. (%)	Total No. (%)
Holding lower employment level compared to pre-immigration status	52 (34.7)	10 (6.7)	62 (41.3)
Holding same or higher level of employment compared to pre-immigration status	38 (25.3)	50 (33.3)	88 (58.7)
Total	90 (60.0)	60 (40.0)	150 (100.0)

and nonbattered women. In terms of participation in clubs and organizations, over one-fourth of the nonbattered women are participating in a Korean association, another one-fourth in social clubs or professional meetings, in contrast to the battered women.

Interestingly, 51 of the battered women are attending Korean churches, while 29 women from the nonbattered group are attending churches and the remaining women of the nonbattered group are participating in a variety of organizations, in contrast to 22 battered women of no membership. It seems that more battered Korean women put emphasis on intimate social relations with fellow Korean women through the ethnic churches where there is a large concentration of Korean immigrants, but they are still battered in spite of their extensive socialization.

It is observed that under circumstances such as the lack of socialization, the majority of Korean women are experiencing a great deal of stress in their daily lives. Hence, the hypothesis that the more stress-factors Korean immigrant women face, the more likely they are to experience wife abuse was substantiated with regard to access to going out, talking to friends and relatives and participation in clubs or other organizations.

Two-Career Families and Traditional Families

Less than 19% of the total 150 cases from the battering group (32% of 90 battered cases), and 13% of the total 150 cases from the nonbattering group (30% of 60 nonbattered cases), were unemployed at the time of the relationship which the women were reporting. This shows that the majority of the respondents' families, both husbands and wives, were employed. This shows no significant differences and battered women and nonbattered women could be said to be similar in this area. ANOVA ANALYSIS also shows the income from the women's employment as not being significant (F = 0.13). Thus, there is no direct link between unemployment and wife abuse for our sample (see Table 16). Other researchers have reported such a relationship (Gelles, 1972; Straus et al., 1980) but it is unknown who was their informant.

Perhaps stress from employment status is being used as a means to rationalize undesirable behavior rather than showing a cause and effect relationship (Walker, 1984). The previous analysis indicated that the majority of Korean women in this

TABLE 16

ANALYSIS OF VARIANCE OF LEVEL OF ABUSE BY RESPONDENTS' EMPLOYMENT STATUS

Source	df	SS	ms	F	P-value
Employment Status	1	360.0972	360.0972	2.28	Not Significant (p >.05)
Error	148	22,782.2967	158.2143		
Total	149	23,142.9589			

study actually bear the heavy burden of performing household tasks. As indicated by research in the Korean community in 1984 (Hurh and Kim), Korean wives are also expected to perform these tasks regardless of their employment status. In this respect, employment of the wife makes no difference; she bears the major responsibility of performing household tasks whether she is currently employed or not. In correspondence to this situation, a substantial proportion of Korean battered wives suffered from stress from both work and performance of the household tasks. Results from the above analysis do not confirm the hypothesis that the level of wife abuse is directly related to the employment status of women.

Korean-Korean Couples and Korean-American Couples

Out of the total thirty-five transculturally (K-A) married women, twenty-three women (65%) reported abusive incidents in their home. For the Korean-Korean married group, 74% (N=67) of the women were reported as battered women. The difference between the two groups was not statistically significant ($x^2 = .62$, $p > .05$, $F = 6.29$, $p > .05$), as shown in Table 17. Although the prevailing impressions derived from various clinical cases indicated the maladjustment of Korean women who were married to American husbands (Kim, 1972), the result from this study does not confirm the more contaminated outlook on an assessment of conjugal relationships among the Korean-American married couples than any other married couples in the Korean immigrant community. Rather, the findings from the present study do not show a difference between the Korean-American married women and Korean-Korean married women. This finding is consistent with the results of research on transculturally married Korean wives and American husbands

TABLE 17

ANALYSIS OF VARIANCE OF LEVEL OF ABUSE BY HUSBANDS' RACIAL BACKGROUND

Source	df	SS	ms	F	P-value
Race Status	1	31.5963	31.5963	6.29	Not Significant (p >.05)
Error	148	421.8920	5.0225		
Total	149	453.4883			

(Lee, 1980) in that the transculturally married American husbands and Korean wives, as a group, did not seem to differ from the general and endogamously married couples in the level of their overall marital adjustment.

However, there was some evidence to suggest insights. The comparison of demographic characteristics between the two groups indicated that there is some difference in regard to their marital status, education and religious affiliation while there are no group differences in terms of length of residence in the United States and income in employment status of battered women from both groups.

Relationships of Stress-Related Symptoms to Wife Abuse

Stress-related symptoms were measured by responses to a twenty-two item screening score which was originally developed in New York City and replicated in the study for Chinese immigrant women. Additionally, two items were used to measure the symptoms with regard to suicide. These self-reported symptoms were assigned a score from zero to four corresponding to the frequencies of symptoms. Scores between sixty-one and ninety-six rated as "high" in stress-related symptoms, and scores between twenty-four and sixty rated as "low." Comparisons of battered and nonbattered groups as shown in Table 18 supported the significant differences of stress-related symptom levels between the two groups as expected.

All of the battered women in the sample reported experiencing at least some stress-related symptoms (i.e., difficulty sleeping, occasional headaches, loss of appetite, etc.). Even though the majority of women could have experienced some symptoms prior to the abusive relationship, there were highly significant differences in the symptoms experienced between the battered women and nonbattered women ($x^2 = 6.17$, $p < .05$; $F = 62.54$, $p < .05$) (see Tables 19 & 20).

The respondents in the battered group scored higher in the direction of severe levels of abuse on the measurement of stress-related symptoms. At the same time, the women in the nonbattered group who scored lower on the abuse scale also scored in the direction of having fewer stress-related symptoms. Results from the above analysis do confirm the hypothesis that the level of wife abuse is directly related to the stress-related symptoms.

TABLE 18

RESPONDENTS' DISTRIBUTIONS ON STRESS-RELATED SYMPTOMS BY BATTERED AND NONBATTERED WOMEN

Scores of Stress-Related Symptoms	Battered Women No. (%)	Nonbattered Women No. (%)	Total No. (%)
High	47 (31.3)	19 (12.7)	66 (44.0)
Low	43 (28.7)	41 (27.3)	84 (56.0)
Total	90 (60.00)	60 (40.0)	150 (100.0)

$x^2 = 6.17$, $p < .05$

TABLE 19

CORRELATION MATRIX: RESPONDENTS' STRESS RELATED SYMPTOMS AND WIFE ABUSE

Abusive Acts	Resultant Injuries	Level of Wife Abuse (Acts & Injuries)	Stress Related Symptoms
Resultant Injuries			
Level of Wife Abuse (Acts & Injuries)	.937 ($p < .05$)		
Stress Related Symptom	.598 ($p < .05$)	.548 ($p < .05$)	

N = 150

TABLE 20

ANALYSIS OF VARIANCE OF LEVEL OF ABUSE BY STRESS-RELATED SYMPTOMS

Source	df	SS	ms	F	Pvalue
Stress-related Status	1	6,968.8023	6,968.8023	62.54	Is Significant ($p < .05$)
Error	148	16,157.0474	111.4297		
Total	149	23,125.8503			

Coping with Wife Abuse

Ninety respondents fall in the battered relationship with their spouse, and the remaining sixty women into the nonbattered category. Sixty percent (N = 90) of Korean women in this study experience some degree of wife abuse in their relationship with their spouse. In this section, we shall be concerned with what our respondents do to cope with abuse in terms of their knowledge of problem-solving methods, service needs, utilization of patterns of sources of help, and barriers to the use of formal services.

Problem-solving methods

The problem-solving methods were assessed by asking the women to check the most preferred methods of solving problems from the five suggested methods. The most preferred ways of problem-solving for the battered women were, respectively: (1) Assuming that time will solve the problem (42%); (2) Keeping the problem in the family (35%); (3) Praying (27%); (4) Consulting friends and relatives (12%); (5) Seeking professional help (5%).

Interestingly, 42% of the battered women indicated that time will solve the problem. As indicated by Lee (1980), this appears to be a cultural pattern of problem-solving methods for Koreans.

Crisis management

In order to identify the patterns in crisis management, a question was asked: When you are in a crisis, where would you go for help? It is interesting to note that over half of the battered women reported they would turn to their husband or minister. They were less likely to turn to their friends, relatives, and neighbors for help. Surprisingly, only 2% of the women indicated they would turn to social service agencies for managing their crises. The majority of women would not seek help from their friends, relatives, or neighbors. As indicated by Koh and Koh (1974), Korean immigrants seem to have less intimate relations with their relatives, friends, or neighbors to whom they can freely ask for help in the crisis situation. The results seem to reveal at least two important findings: one, many battered women (N = 48) managed their crisis situations by seeking help from their own abusive spouses; and two, there is evidence of tremendous underutilization of social service agencies by Korean women.

Only 17% of the battered women had sought professional help at some time, while another three-quarters of the battered women had not had contact with any professional. Of the three battered women who had contacted the police because of the violence, all of them were cases where their neighbors called the police. Four battered women had seen a Korean internist for treatment of injuries due to battering, three women had consulted an attorney for legal services, and five battered Korean women had received services by social workers.

Knowledge of formal services

Respondents' knowledge of formal services was obtained through their friends (10%), Korean newspapers (8%), Korean church (4%), a social service agency (2%), and the Korean community center (6%). These results indicate another 70% of the battered women were not aware of formal services at the time of the interview. One-third of the battered women indicated they did not know where to go. On the other hand, close to one-fifth of the battered women indicated they were not aware of formal services because of English, 12% were not interested, and 6% indicated they did not have any problem to solve. Furthermore, respondents were asked to identify the barriers to the use of formal services. A question was asked: If you know of formal sources of help and need to seek help, yet do not utilize those sources, what stops you from using those services?

It is not surprising that close to three-quarters of the women considered it shameful to admit the situation to friends and neighbors, and another 65% indicated language problems as one of the major barriers to the use of formal services. Forty-six battered women (51%) indicated they did not know how to approach such services while thirty-four women indicated family rejection as a barrier, and twenty-one women cited transportation problems.

Would a mother nurse a child
who does not cry aloud?

Korean Proverb

CHAPTER 7

Summary and Conclusions

The major purpose of this study was to investigate whether Korean immigrant women could be significantly affected by cultural conflict during their adjustment period in terms of the abuse in their homes.

Summary

On review of the hypotheses, testings, and results, the following conclusions on this research can be summarized:

1. Characteristics of the abuse were identified in groups. They included abusive acts, injuries, precipitating arguments, reactive response to abuse, and behavior after abusive incidents. It was found that 60% of Korean women experienced wife abuse. The resultant injuries varied from black eyes to physical injury requiring hospitalization.

Unlike research on American battered women (Carlson, 1977; Gelles, 1972; Walker, 1979; Roy, 1977; Martin, 1979; and Gayford, 1975), the present study found drinking problems and problems related to love life to be much less important as causes of argument than in American families. Furthermore, the present study differed considerably from Hofeller's research (1982) on American battered women in that 50% of the American women reported they had fought back physically, in contrast to the women in this study, who showed a nonassertive-to-passive reaction to abuse.

2. Battered Korean women did not differ significantly from those who were not battered on the demographical variables studied except in length of residence, marital status, and living arrangements. This shows a disparity between the current study and research on American battered women with regard to their demographical variables.

For example, there are good indications in research on American families that certain demographical backgrounds affect wife abuse, such as income, education, and employment (Gelles, 1972; Prescott & Letko, 1977; Roy, 1977). However, the results show no significant relationship between the above variables and wife abuse; rather, it is not yet possible to identify one set of demographics which can differentiate between battered and nonbattered women. However, it appears to be directly related to length of residence, that is, the time spent adjusting to the culture of America, and the problems arising in childrearing in a new culture as described earlier.

3. Results from the current study suggested that Korean women with more traditional attitudes experience more abuse than women who are less traditional. It could be argued that the tradition of tolerance and endurance in Korean culture is one aspect of the possible causal factor in wife abuse among Korean immigrants. Results clearly indicated that there was a positive correlation between women's attitudes toward Korean traditionalism and the level of wife abuse.

Most battered Korean women try to fulfill traditional images of good wives. In short, they tend to see themselves primarily as wives and mothers rather than as individuals and believe that they should be submissive and forgiving of their spouse's abuse. Furthermore, "traditional" wives tend to view the relative success of their marriages as a reflection of their worth as human beings (Hofeller, 1982). Therefore, they view "leaving an abusive husband" as threatening in terms of economics and social stigma, as well as evidence of personal failure.

4. The results of the present study indicate that there is evidence to suggest that couples who adhere to a rigid Korean sex role performance are more violent than couples who are less rigid. The Korean man who beats his wife tends to adhere to a rigid stereotyped model of normative Korean masculine behavior, a role requiring that he do hardly any household tasks and make all important family decisions.

The batterer may also expect his wife to fulfill a rigid sex role as well. The battered Korean women are found to be responsible for all household chores. Because the batterer is already insecure, the most innocuous of actions may be perceived as a threat to his "male ego." For example, a Korean man might hit his wife because she did not have dinner ready when he came home, or left dirty dishes in the kitchen sink when she had to rush to go to work, or failed to do laundry on some occasion, etc.

5. There was significant evidence to indicate that stress-evoking factors affect the level of wife abuse. For instance, language problems and social isolation are frequently associated with episodes of battering. The language problems of some Koreans severely limit their cultural and social activities. Language problems and social isolation are well known as a major obstacle (Yu, 1977; Koh and Koh, 1974; Lee, 1980), causing frustration for Koreans in the process of making a new life in the United States. Especially social isolation of battered women, due to the lack of sociability, has been written about in the literature as occurring both as a part of and as a result of violence. It has been suggested that the abuser systematically isolates the woman from others, and that she also withdraws to protect herself from further embarrassment (Walker, 1979; Martin, 1979).

The battered women in this study were not likely to be involved in voluntary organizations, other than churches. Although it was not possible to devise a measure for a Christian woman's reason for staying in an abusive relationship, results from interviewing these women do suggest that women who belonged to those churches tended to endure more. Therefore, attending Korean churches may actually contribute to ethnic segregation and to further social isolation. This is only suggestive of the relative importance of determining the possible causal factor contributing to wife abuse. Other stresses, such as status inconsistency of couples in employment compared to preimmigration status, are found to be indicators in predicting greater occurrences of wife abuse in the Korean family.

6. There was no significant difference in the level of abuse occurring in two-career families and traditional families. As indicated in earlier research (Hurh, Kim and Kim, 1979; and Koh and Koh, 1974), high participation in the labor market among Korean immigrant families compared to their preimmigration employment status is consistent with the results of this study. The results showed that the majority of the Korean women (who previously just stayed at home in Korea) were employed since immigration to the United States. However, there is no direct link between unemployment and wife abuse for our sample. In comparison to the situation of battered employed women, a substantial proportion of these women suffered stress from their work and from household tasks. Perhaps their double responsibility may be a precipitating (or facilitating) factor of wife abuse rather than employment status itself.

7. There was no significant difference in the level of abuse occurring in Korean-Korean couples and Korean-American couples. The difference between the two groups was not statistically significant in relation to wife abuse. However, the comparison of demographic characteristics between the two groups indicated that there are some differences in regard to their marital status, education, and religious affiliation.

8. Difference between the stress-related symptom levels of battered and nonbattered Korean women was highly significant, even considering that some of the battered women's symptoms may have had no relation to wife abuse. Although it was not possible to identify different types of symptoms both prior to the abuse and during the battering situations, results indicated that abused women clearly experienced severe stress-related symptoms ranging from loss of appetite to attempted suicide.

9. In reviewing the patterns in crisis management and problem-solving methods reported by the battered Korean women, we find significant evidence of underutilization of any professional help. Close to half of the battered women in this study indicated that they felt time would resolve their problems. In a crisis situation, the battered Korean women in this study reported that their own abusive husbands were the primary resource person they turned to for help.

The majority of women are hesitant to discuss their problem or to approach friends, relatives, or neighbors. The results show the majority of battered women were not aware of formal services, that they did not know where to go or were not interested or felt that the language barrier blocked them from using services of social agencies. Furthermore, the majority of battered Korean women considered that seeking help from a formal source would shame them in front of friends and neighbors. The battered women indicated that they did not know how to approach an agency nor how to communicate well enough to obtain help or that they faced family rejection.

Suggestions for Future Study

Results of the present study suggest that there are a number of issues which should be investigated more fully. To begin with, since this study is the first on Korean battered women, it is suggested this research be replicated in other urban areas of the United States with a larger sample of women.

Second, it would be valuable to investigate Korean battered women still living in Korea to learn the differences and similarities in level of abuse, problem-solving patterns, and other possible causal factors.

Third, studies should focus on the pre-battering stage of abusive relationships. The data could be compared to a similar period in nonbattered couples, thereby providing ways of identifying patterns of interaction associated with wife abuse.

Fourth, future research should be designed to investigate the relationship between the battered women and her children. It should be noted how the battered woman's lack of confidence and self-worth affect her parenting.

Fifth, information is needed regarding the character and quality of childhood experiences of both batterers and the battered woman, as well as of nonbattered couples. It is necessary to compare battered and nonbattered couples on several variables directed toward specifying the childhood experience of growing up in the context of Korean culture.

Finally, since research has indicated that wife abuse is a widespread phenomenon among the Korean immigrant population, it is suggested that future studies include American-American couples, so as to allow a comparison of the two groups.

Conclusion

Throughout this study, the term "battered" did not include verbal abuse. Even though this is undeniably damaging and painful, the overall consensus of feeling among Korean women of the present study was that the verbal abuse is not actually wife abuse. In this respect, there must be a hidden percentage of battered (abused) women in the Korean immigrant population in addition to the 60% revealed in this study. This estimation shows a great contrast to the cases of wife abuse in American homes. Where there is some level of wife abuse, about 50 percent included verbal and psychological abuse (Straus, 1976). Just reviewing the significant underutilization of services tells us that these battered Korean women are still hidden from societal attention, and they hardly talk about problems with anybody. Their fear is that talking about the wife abuse in too much detail will cause further harm. Nevertheless, most of the battered Korean women in this study did remember the details of the abuse and could relate it when asked direct and specific questions. Most women did report the battering incidents as though they were recalling them.

In spite of the emotions and anxieties which the interview aroused, however, many women said that they had felt talking about the abuse had been greatly beneficial, especially those who had kept it to themselves for years and years without telling anybody. It was not unusual for a woman to say that she had gained new insight and a better understanding of her situation. It appeared that, although actual counseling was not provided, the discussion of wife abuse in an accepting, nonjudgmental setting was indeed therapeutic as indicated in other research (Walker, 1984; Hofeller, 1982).

The findings and observations of the study pose a challenge to the community to provide appropriate services for these battered women. The fact that very few Korean women sought professional help indicates not only that the cultural pattern of Korean immigrants rejects the idea of professional help, but also that there must be many untreated, unrevealed cases in the Korean populations in the major urban places in the United States, and extending also to other Asian women. They are facing language barriers, cultural differences, myths, and stereotypes. Therefore, they are in even greater risk in their current situation and in more need of professional help.

The better provision of services for Korean women requires specifically focused programs on wife abuse in general and specifically targeted programs for concentrated areas of the Korean population in particular.

Public education should be geared toward specific objectives. There must be a consciousness raising in the Korean immigrant community about the extent and nature of wife abuse. At the same time, battered women themselves need to be reached through counseling agencies, public services, and the media (Korean newspapers and radio programs). Korean battered women need to realize that they should not feel guilty or embarrassed about this problem, and that there is help available. For example, communities could distribute handbooks containing information on the myths and stereotypes about wife abuse and also provide resources written in both English and Korean. On the other hand, the violent Korean husbands must somehow be reached. They must be informed that they have no right to abuse their wives. In addition, since abusive men are typically reluctant to seek help, the message should include the idea that it is not weak or unmasculine to get help for this problem. It might be helpful for a professional volunteer group of men to undertake such a task and provide male counselors (Hofeller, 1982).

We as a society still give informal sanction to wife abuse in the Korean immigrant community. For example, current myths about "quiet," "nonproblematic," "self-managing" Asian Americans including Korean immigrants tend to cover and minimize the problems faced by Korean immigrants. In addition to this is the myth that wifebeating is a lower-class phenomenon. Contrary to these beliefs, the present study showed that regardless of the respondent's education and income level, wife beating occurs in Korean couples. The present myths about wife abuse tend to make the battered women feel ashamed and avoid seeking help and also cause others to view them as undeserving of help. There is a tendency to believe that the Korean woman is battered because she "did something wrong." Therefore, others often do not want to help a woman who chooses to be mistreated. The battered Korean woman herself may also come to believe this myth. Regardless of what she truly thinks, she may begin to suspect that perhaps she really did something wrong. This increases her shame and makes it even less likely she will tell anyone about the abuse occurring behind closed doors. On the other hand, it might appear that the problem with violent Korean husbands is that they are too aggressive. However, many Korean husbands who are violent in their own homes may be quite passive in other situations.

By contrast, the batterer may not speak up when he feels exploited. Especially it may be significant for this study that 52 violent Korean husbands out of a total of 90 batterers are holding lower employment levels compared to their pre-immigration status. It is not unusual to find many Korean men with years of professional training, such as doctors, lawyers, etc., holding clerical positions or even manual types of jobs due to the difficulties in licensing and language and cultural barriers. These husbands have a great deal of frustration, keeping this anger "bottled-up" inside until they get home. Then they may overreact with violence to the slightest threat to their status (Hofeller, 1982). Furthermore, as Hofeller indicated, a truly assertive person is not aggressive. Instead, he stands up for his rights without running "roughshod" over the rights of others, especially those of his own wife. Rather, assertive communication should be based on a strong sense of respect for oneself and for others.

Thus, the implication for child rearing requires the attention of these Korean immigrant families. The child who is raised to be assertive learns that he does not have to use violence in order to show his rights or fulfill his needs. At the same time, if an "assertive" woman believes she has been taken advantage of, she can talk about those feelings at the time. It is obvious she realizes her right to demand a nonabusive relationship and can do what is needed to make sure she is not abused. However, entire communities should accept and encourage Korean women to be assertive and independent, and men should be able to express the more tender, sensitive, and nondominant side. From this respect, if these Korean couples could react to each other first, as person to person, and then as male or female, they would, one hopes, begin to interact with each other with better understanding and with fewer incidences of wife abuse.

REFERENCES

Allen, C. M., and Straus, M. A. 1980. "Resources, Power and Husband-Wife Violence." In M. A. Straus and G. T. Hotaling, eds., *The Social Causes of Husband-Wife Violence*. Minneapolis: University of Minnesota Press.

Amir, Y. 1969. "Birth Order, Family Structure, and Avoidance Behavior." *Journal of Personality and Social Psychology*. 10.

Ball, M. 1977. "Issues of Violence in Family Casework." *Social Casework* . 8.

Bandura, A. 1973. *Aggression: A Social Learning Analysis*. Englewood Cliffs, New Jersey: Prentice-Hall.

Bandura, A., Ross, O., and Ross, S. A. 1961. "Transmission of Aggression Through Imitation of Aggressive Models." *Journal of Abnormal and Social Psychology* . 63.

Beauvoir, Simone de. 1953. *The Second Sex*. Translated and edited by H. M. Parshley. New York: Knopf.

Berkowitz, L. 1962. *Aggression: A Social Psychological Analysis*. New York: Free Press.

_______. 1969. "The Frustration-Aggression Hypothesis Revisited." In L. Berkowitz, ed., *Roots of Aggression*. New York: Atherton.

Berlinger, B. 1958. "The Role of Object Relations in Mortal Masochism." *Psychoanalytic Quarterly* . 27.

Blau, P. M. 1964. *Exchange and Power in Social Life*. New York: Wiley.

Bogardus, Emory S. 1968. "Comparing Racial Distance in Ethiopia, South Africa and the United States." *Sociology and Social Research.* 52.

Bonaparte, M. 1965. *Female Sexuality.* New York: Grove Press.

Brandt, Vincent S. R. 1971. *A Korean Village Between Farm and Sea.* Cambridge, Mass.: Harvard University Press.

Buss, A. H. 1971. "Aggression Pays." In J. L. Singer, ed.,*The Control of Aggression and Violence.* New York: Academic Press.

Carlson, Bonnie E. 1977. "Battered Women and Their Assailants." *Social Work.* November.

Chafe, William. 1976. "Looking Backward in Order to Look Forward: Women, Work, and Social Values in America." In Juanita Kreps, ed.,*Women and the American Economy: A Look to the 1980's.* Englewood Cliffs, New Jersey: Prentice-Hall.

Chapman, Jan Roberts. 1978. "The Economics of Women's Victimization." In Chapman and Gates, eds., *Victimization of Women.* Beverly Hills: Sage Publications.

Choi, Jai-Suek. 1977. "Family System." *Korea Journal.* 17.

_______. 1966. *A Study of the Korean Family.* Seoul: Minjung-sogwan (In Korean, with title and summary in English).

Choy, Bong-youn. 1979. *Koreans in America*. Chicago: Nelson Hall.

Chung, S. H. 1980. "Korean Culture and Mental Health." In John McDermott, Jr. et al., eds., *People and Cultures of Hawaii*. Honolulu: University Press of Hawaii.

Chung, S. H., and Rieckelman, A. 1974. "The Koreans of Hawaii." In J. McDermott, Jr. and T. Maretzki, eds., *People and Cultures in Hawaii*. Honolulu: University Press of Hawaii.

Crane, Paul. 1967. *Korean Patterns*. Seoul, Korea: Hollym Corporation.

D'Andrade, R. C. 1966. "Sex Differences and Cultural Institutions." In E. E. Maccoby, ed., *The Development of Sex Differences*. Stanford University Press.

Davidson, T. 1977. "Wifebeating: A Recurring Phenomenon." In M. Roy, ed., *Battered Women-- A Psychosociological Study of Domestic Violence*. New York: Van Nostrand Reinhold Company.

_______. 1978. *Conjugal Crime: Understanding and Changing Wife Beating Patterns*. New York: Hawthorn Books, Inc.

Deutsch, H. 1944-1945. *The Psychology of Women: A Psychoanalytic Interpretation*. New York: Grune and Stratton.

Dhooper, S., and Tran, T. 1986. "Social Work with Asian Americans." Paper presented at the 32nd Council on Social Work Education Annual Program Meeting. Miami, Florida.

Dobash, R. E., and Dobash, R. P. 1979. *Violence Against Wives.* New York: The Free Press.

Dollard, J.; Doob, L. W.; Miller, N. E.; Mowrer, O. H.; and Seals, R. R. 1939. *Frustration and Aggression.* New Haven, CT.: Yale University Press.

The Dong-A-Ilbo. "Korean Immigrant Couples." 4/22/75.

Feldman, S. E. 1983. "Battered Women: Psychological Correlates of the Victimization Process." Ph.D. dissertation, Department of Psychology, Ohio State University.

Fink, S. L. 1967. "Crisis and Motivation: A Theoretical Model." *Archives of Physical Medicine and Rehabilitation.* 48.

Firestone, Shulamith. 1970. *The Dialectic of Sex: The Case for Feminist Revolution.* New York: William Morrow and Co., Inc.

Flynn, John P. 1977. "Recent Findings Related to Wife Abuse." *Social Casework.* January.

Freeman, J., ed., 1979. *Women: A Feminist Perspective,* 2nd Ed. Palo Alto, CA: Mayfield Publishing Company.

Freud, S. 1949-1950. "The Economic Problem in Masochism." In E. Jones and J. Riviere eds., *Collected Papers,* vol. II. London: Hogarth Press. (Originally published, 1924).

Ganley, A., and Harris, L. 1979. "Treatment of Batterers: An Overview." Paper presented at Northwest Women's Action on Family Violence Conference. Tacoma, Washington.

Gayford, J. 1975. "Wife Battering: A Preliminary Survey of 100 Cases." *British Medical Journal*. January.

Gelles, R. J. 1972. *The Violent Home-- A Study of Physical Aggression Between Husbands and Wives*. Beverly Hills: Sage Publications.

_______. 1973. "Child Abuse as Psychopathology: A Sociological Critique and Reformation." *American Journal of Orthopsychiatry*. 45.

_______. 1975. "Violence and Pregnancy: A Note on the Extent of the Problem and Needed Services." *Family Coordinator*. 24.

Gies, F., and Gies, J. 1978. *Women in the Middle Ages*. New York: Thomas Y. Crowell Company.

Goode, W. J. 1973. "Violence Between Intimates." In William Goode, ed., *Exploration Social Theory*. New York: Oxford University Press.

_______. 1974. "Force and Violence in the Family." In S.K. Steinmetz and M. A. Straus, eds., *Violence in the Family*. New York: Harper & Row.

Gutmacher, M. 1960. *The Mind of the Murder*. New York: Farrar, Straus, and Cudahy.

Han-Kook Daily News. "Expansion of Korean Churches." 4/21/83:9.

Harvey, Young Sook. 1980. "The Koreans." In John McDermott, Jr. et al., eds., *People and Cultures of Hawaii*. Honolulu, HI: The University Press of Hawaii.

_______. 1979. *Six Korean Women.* St. Paul, Minnesota: West Publishing Company.

Hiroto, D. 1974. "Locus of Control and Learned Helplessness." *Journal of Experimental Psychology.* 102.

Hofeller, H. Kathleen. 1982. *Social, Psychological and Situational Factors in Wife Abuse.* Palo Alto, CA: R & E Research Associates, Inc.

Homes, T. H., and Rahe, R. H. 1967. "The Social Readjustment Rating Scale." *Journal of Psychosomatic Research.* 11.

Hong, Kay, and Shin, Myong-Sop. 1975. *The Korean Immigrants in Hawaii, 1970-1974: A Study of Their Problems.* Honolulu: Immigrant Service Center.

Horney, K. 1967. "The Problem of Feminine Masochism." In H. Kelman, ed., *Feminine Psychology.* New York: W. W. Norton and Company, Inc.

Hoyos, A.; Hoyos; and Anderson. 1986. "Sociocultural Dislocation: Beyond the Dual Perspective." *Social Work.* 31.

Hurh, W. M., and Kim, K. C. 1984. *Korean Immigrants in America: A Structural Analysis of Ethnic Confinement and Adhesive Adaptation.* Cranberry, NJ: Association of University Presses.

_______. 1988. "Uprooting and Adjustments: A Sociological Study of Migration and Mental Health." A final report for the National Institute for Mental Health. Macomb, Illinois: Western Illinois University.

Hurh, Won Moo. 1977. *Comparative Study of Korean Immigrants in the U.S.* San Francisco: R and E Research Associates.

Hurh, Won Moo; Kim, Hei Chu; and Kim, Kwang Chung. 1979. *Assimilation Patterns of Immigrants in the United States: A Case Study of Korean Immigrants in the Chicago Area.* Washington, D.C.: University Press of America.

Ishisaka, H., and Takagi, C. 1982. "Social work with Asian and Pacific Americans." In J. Green, ed., *Cultural Awareness in the Human Services.* Englewood Cliffs, New Jersey: Prentice-Hall, Inc.

Kalish, R., and Yuen, S. 1971. "Americans of East Asian Ancestry: Aging and the Aged." *The Gerontologist.* 11.

Kalton, Michael, C. 1979. "Korean Ideas and Values." In Philip Memorial Paper Number 7. Elkins Park, Pennsylvania: Philip Memorial Foundation, Inc.

Kim, B. L. 1972. "Casework with Japanese and Korean Wives of Americans." *Social Casework.* 53.

_______. 1978a. "Korean Wives of American Servicemen." *The Hookook Il-Bo.* August.

_______. 1978b. "Pioneers in Intermarriage: Korean Women in the United States." In H. Sunoo and D. S. Kim, eds., *Korean Women in a Struggle for Humanization*. Memphis, Tennessee: Christian Scholars Publication.

Kim, Dong-Soo. 1977. "How They Fared in American Homes: A Follow-up Study of Adopted Korean Children." *Children Today*. 6.

_______. 1978. "From Women to Women with Painful Love: A Study of Maternal Motivation in Intercountry Adoption Process." In H. Sunoo and D. S. Kim, eds., *Korean Women in a Struggle for Humanization*. Memphis, Tennessee: Christian Scholars Publication.

_______. 1978. "Sexuality, Womanhood, and Humanization from Socio-Psychophysiological Perspectives." In H. Sunoo and D. S. Kim, eds., *Korean Women in a Struggle for Humanization*. Memphis, Tennessee: Christian Scholars Publication.

Kim, Eugene. 1990. "Korean Americans in the United States: Problems and Alternatives." In H.C. Kim and E.H. Lee, eds., *Koreans in America: Dreams and Realities*. Seoul: The Institute of Korean Studies.

Kim Hei Chu; Kim, Kwang Chun; and Hurh, Won Moo. 1979. "Ethnic Roles of the Korean Church in the Chicago Area." In P. Nandi, E. Yu, and W. Liu, eds., *Asian Americans: Identity, Adaptation and Survival*. Nashville, TN: Charter House.

Kim, Hyon-Ja. 1971. "The Changing Role of Women in Korea." *Korea Journal*. 11.

Kim, Hyung-Chan. 1977. "Korean Community Organizations in America: Their Characteristics and Problems." In Hyung-Chan Kim, ed., *The Korean Diaspora*. Santa Barbara: ABC-Clio Press.

_______. 1990. "Korean Christian Churches in the Pacific Northwest: Resources for Korean Ethnic Identity?" In H.C. Kim and E.H. Lee, eds., *Koreans in America: Dreams and Realities*. Seoul: The Institute of Korean Studies.

Kim, Jung Ki. 1978. "Some Value Questions for Ethnic Orientation: An Ethnical Perspective on Korean Immigration Motives." In Myongsup Shin et al., eds., *Korean Immigrants in Hawaii*. Honolulu, HI: Bess Press.

Kim, K. C., and Hurh, W. M. 1983. "Korean Americans and the 'Success' Image: A Critique." *Amerasia Journal*. 10.

Kim, Paul, and Brown, F. 1985. "Asian Americans in the United States: Implications for Social Work Education." Paper presented at the 30th Council on Social Work Education, Washington D.C.

Kim, Young-Chung. 1976. *Women of Korea: A History From Ancient Times to 1945*. Edited and Translated by The Committee for the Compilation of the History of Korean Women. Seoul: Ewha Women's University Press.

Kitano, Harry L. 1967. "Japanese Crime and Delinquency." *Journal of Psychology*. 66.

Kitano, Harry L., and Stanley, Sue. 1973. "The Model Minorities." *The Journal of Social Issues*. 23.

Koh, Kwang-Lim, and Koh, Hesung, C., ed., 1974. *Koreans and Korean-Americans in the United States: A Summary of Three Conference Proceedings*. New Haven, CT.: East Rock.

The Korean Times. "Wife Beating in Korean Immigrant Homes." 9/20/85: 5.

_______. "Relationship Between Conjugal Violence and Health." 4/21/83: 9.

_______. "Phenomenon of Wife Abuse and Child Abuse in Korean Immigrant Homes." 8/7/93.

_______. "Koreans in America." 4/6/93.

Kubler-Ross, E., ed., 1975. *Death: The Final Stage of Growth*. Englewood Cliffs, NJ: Prentice-Hall.

Kwon, Peter. 1975. "Report on the Needs of Korean Community and Churches in the United States." A paper presented at Asian American Presbyterian Caucus in Southern California. July.

Langley, R., and Levy, R. 1978. *Wife Beating--the Silent Crisis*. New York: Simon and Schuster.

Lee, B. S. 1966. *Chosenno Kongingho* [The Marriage and Divorce Laws of Korea]. Tokyo: Syopung Kwan.

Lee, Daniel B. 1984. "An Epidemiological Appraisal of Asian Students, Staff and Faculty at The Ohio State University." Research Monograph, The Ohio State University.

_______. 1980. "Military Transitional Marriage: A Study of Marital Adjustment Between American Husbands and Korean-born Spouses." DSW dissertation at the University of Utah.

Lee, Don Chang. 1975. *Acculturation of Korean Residents in Georgia.* San Francisco: R and E Research Associates.

Lee, Hyo-Je. 1973. "Changing Korean Family and the Old." *Korean Journal.* 13.

_______. 1990. "New Family Structure in Changing Society." In T. Lee and W. Lee, eds., *Hyon Dae Hankook Yo Sung Ran* [Modern Korean Women]. Seoul: Sam Min Sin So.

_______. 1989. *Hankook Yosung Undong* [The Status of Korean Women]. Seoul: Jung Woo Press.

Lee, In-Ho. 1977. "Women's Liberation in Korea." *Korea Journal.* 17.

Lee, O. Young. 1967. *In This Earth and in That Wind: This Is Korea.* David I. Steinberg, trans. Seoul: Hollym Corp.

Lee, Sang Hyun. 1979. "The Meaning of Marginality: Toward a Theology of Immigration." A paper presented at the Annual Meeting at AKCS in Boston.

Lee, T. 1981. *The Legal Status of Korean Women.* Seoul: Ewha Press.

Lorenzo, M.K., and Adler, D. A. 1984. "Mental Health Services for Chinese in a Community Health Center." *Social Casework*. 65.

Mace, Vera, and Mace, D. 1959. *Marriage: East and West*. Garden City, NY: Doubleday and Co., Inc.

Martin, D. 1983. *Battered Wives*. New York: Pocket Books.

______. 1979. "What Keeps a Woman Captive in a Violent Relationship." In Donna Moore, ed., *Battered Women*. Beverly Hills, CA: Sage Publications.

McWilliams. 1964. *Brothers Under the Skin*. Boston: Little, Brown and Co.

Mead, M. and MacGregor, C. 1951. *Growth and Culture: A Photographic Study of Balinese Children*. New York: Putnam.

Mill, J. S. 1970. *The Subjection of Women*. London: Longmans, Green and Co.

Miller, N. E. 1969. "The Frustration-Aggression Hypothesis." *Psychological Review*. 48. Reprinted in L. Berkowitz, ed., *Roots of Aggression*. New York: Atherton.

Millett, Kate. 1971. *Sexual Politics*. New York: Avon Books.

Min, P. G. 1988. "Korean Immigrant Entrepreneurship: A Comprehensive Explanation." In S. H. Lee and T. H. Kwak, eds., *Koreans in North America*. Seoul: Kyungnam University Press.

Mokuau, N., and Matsuoka, J. 1986. "The Appropriateness of Practice Theories for Working with Asian and Pacific Islanders." Paper presented at the 32nd Council of Social Work Education Annual Program Meeting. Miami, Florida.

Moon, D.Y. 1978. "Ministering to Korean Wives of Servicemen." In H. Sunoo and D. S. Kim, eds., *Korean Women in a Struggle for Humanization*. Memphis, TN: Christian Scholars Publication.

Moose, J. Robert. 1911. *Village Life in Korea*. Nashville, TN.: Publishing House of the M.E. Church.

Murphy, H. 1978. *Mental Health Trends in the Pacific Islands*. Nomia, New Caledonia: South Pacific Commission.

Nielson, J. M.; Eberly, P.; Thoennes, N.; and Walker, L. 1979. "Why Women Stay in Battering Relationships: Preliminary Results." Presented at the American Sociological Society Meeting. Boston, Massachusetts.

O'Brien, J. E. 1971. "Violence in Divorce Prone Families." *Journal of Marriage and the Family*. 33.

Osgood, Cornelius. 1951. *The Koreans and Their Culture*. New York: Ronald Press.

Overmier, J. G., and Seligman, M. E. 1967. "Effects of Inescapable Shock upon Subsequent Escape and Avoidance Learning." *Journal of Comparative and Physiological Psychology*. 63.

Owens, D. M., and Straus, M. A. 1975. "The Social Structure of Violence in Childhood and Approval of Violence as an Adult." *Aggressive Behavior*. 1.

Palmer, S. 1962. *The Psychology of Murder*. New York: Thomas Y. Crowell.

Parker, E., and Schumacher, D. 1977. "The Battered Wife Syndrome and Violence in the Nuclear Family of Origin: A Controlled Pilot Study." *American Journal of Public Health*. 67.

Parkes, C. M. 1972. *Bereavement: Studies of Grief in Adult Life*. New York: International Universities Press.

Ponce, D. 1974. "The Filipinos of Hawaii." In W. Tseng, J. McDermott, Jr., and T. Maretzki, eds., *Peoples and Culture of Hawaii*. Hawaii: Department of Psychiatry, University of Hawaii.

Prescott, S. L., and Letko, C. 1977. "Battered Women-- A Social Psychological Perspective." In M. Roy, ed., *Battered Women-- A Psychosociological Study of Domestic Violence*. New York: Van Nostrand Reinhold Co.

Rhim, S. M. 1978. "The Status of Women in Traditional Korean Society." In H. Sunoo and D. S. Kim, eds., *Women in a Struggle for Humanization*. Memphis, TN: Christian Scholars Publications.

Roy, M. 1977. "A Current Survey of 150 Cases." In M. Roy, ed., *Battered Women--A Psychosociological Study of Domestic Violence*. New York: Van Nostrand Reinhold Co.

Rutt, Richard. 1967. *Korean Works and Days*. Tokyo: Charles E. Tuttle Co. Inc.

Ryan, W. 1976. *Blaming the Victim..* New York: Vintage Books.

Ryu, J. P. 1977. "Koreans in America: A Demographic Analysis." In Hyung-Chan Kim, ed., *The Korean Diaspora.* Santa Barbara: ABC-Clio Press.

Sanders, Daniel. 1978. "Social Policies and Welfare Issues in Relation to Korean Immigrants." In Myong Sup Shin, ed., *Korean Immigrants in Hawaii.* University of Hawaii: Bess Press.

Scanzoni, J. H. 1972. *Sexual Bargaining.* Englewood Cliffs, NJ: Prentice-Hall.

Schnepp, G. J., and Yu, A. M. 1955. "Cultural and Marital Adjustment of Japanese War Brides." *American Journal of Sociology.* 61.

Schultz, LeRoy. 1960. "The Wife Assaulter." *Corrective Psychiatry and Journal of Social Therapy.* 6 (2).

Seligman, M. E., and Maier, S. F. 1967. "Failure to Escape Traumatic Shock." *Journal of Experimental Psychology.* 74 (1).

Shainess, N. 1977. "Logical Aspects of Wife Battery." In *Battered Women: A Psychosociological Study of Domestic Violence.* New York: Van Nostrand Reinhold.

Shin, Linda. 1971. "Koreans in America." In Amy Tachiki, et al. eds., *Roots: An Asian American Reader.* Los Angeles: Continental Graphics.

Shin, Myong Sup. 1978. *Korean Immigrants in Hawaii.* Honolulu, HI: Beau Press.

Singer, J. L., ed., 1971. *The Control of Aggression and Violence.* New York: Academic Press.

Snell, J. E., Rosenwals, R. J., and Robey, A. 1964. "The Wifebeater's Wife: A Study of Family Interaction." *Archives of General Psychiatry.* 11.

Son, Dug-Soo. 1978. "The Status of Korean Women from the Perspective of the Women's Emancipation Movement in Korean Women." In H. Sunoo and D.S. Kim, eds., *Women in a Struggle for Humanization.* Memphis, TN: Christian Scholars Publications.

Song, Young. 1982. "A Report on Korean Mental Health Needs Assessment." A paper submitted to State Department of Health, Mental Health Division, Honolulu, Hawaii.

_______. 1991. "Single Asian American Women as a Result of a Divorce." *Journal of Divorce & Remarriage.* 14.

_______. 1992. "A Study of Asian Immigrant Women Undergoing Postpartum Depression." In D. Gabaccia, ed., *Seeking Common Ground: Multidisciplinary Studies of Immigrant Women in the United States.* Westport: Greenword Press.

_______. 1992. "Battered Korean Women in Urban United States." In S. Furuto, R. Biswas, D. Chung, K. Murase and F. Russ-Sheriff, ed., *Social Work Practice With Asian Americans.* Newbury Park: Sage Publications.

Spinetta, J. J., and Rigler, D. 1972. "The Child-abusing Parent: A Psychological Review." *Psychological Bulletin.* 77.

Stark, R., and McEvoy, J., III. 1970. "Middle Class Violence." *Psychology Today.* November.

Steele, B. F., and Pollock, C. B. 1974. "A Psychiatric Study of Parents Who Abuse Infants and Small Children." In R. E. Helfer and C. H. Kempe, eds., *The Battered Child.* Chicago: University of Chicago Press.

Straus, Murray. 1976. "Sexual Inequality, Cultural Norms and Wife Beating." *Victimology.* Spring.

Straus, M. A. 1977. "Wife Beating: How Common and Why?" *Victimology*, 2 (3-4), 443-459.

Straus, M. A., and Gelles, R. J. 1986. "Societal Change in Family Violence from 1975 to 1985 as Revealed by Two National Surveys." *Journal of Marriage and the Family.* 48.

Straus, M. A.; Gelles, R. J.; and Steinmetz, S. K. 1980. *Behind Closed Doors: Violence in the American Family.* Garden City, NY: Anchor/Doubleday.

Sue, S., and McKinney, H. 1975. "Asian Americans in the Community Mental Health Care System." *American Journal of Orthopsychiatry.* 45.

Theodorson, G., and Theodorson, A. 1969. *A Modern Dictionary of Sociology.* NY: Thomas Y. Crowell Co.

Thoennes, Nancy, A. 1981. "Social Network Functioning Among Battered Women: The Consequences of Geographic Mobility." Dissertation, University of Denver.

Tung, T. M. 1980. "The Indochinese Refugee Mental Health Problem." Department of Psychiatry and Behavioral Science, George Washington University Clinic, Washington, D.C.

United States Department of Justice, 1970-1976 *Annual Report of the Immigration and Naturalization Service*. Washington, D.C.: Department of Justice.

Waites, E. A. 1977-78. "Female Masochism and the Enforced Restriction of Choice." *Victimology: An International Journal*. 2.

Walker, L.E. 1977-78. "Battered Women and Learned Helplessness." *Victimology: An International Journal*. 2.

_______. 1979. *The Battered Woman*. New York: Harper and Row.

_______. 1984. *The Battered Woman Syndrome*. New York: Springer Publishing Co.

Williams, J. H. 1977. "Sexual Role Identification and Level of Functioning in Girls." *Journal of Personality*. 41.

Wolfgang, M.E. 1958. *Patterns in Criminal Homicide*. Philadelphia: The University of Pennsylvania Press.

Wolfgang, M. E., and Ferracuti, F. 1967. *The Subculture of Violence: Towards an Integrated Theory in Criminology*. London: Tavistock Publications Limited.

Wong, M. G., and Hirschman C. 1983. "Labor Force Participation and Socioeconomic Attainment of Asian-American Women." *Sociological Perspectives.* 26.

Yim, Sun Bin. 1978. "Korean Battered Wives: A Sociological and Psychological Analysis of Conjugal Violence in Korean Immigrant Families." In Harold Sunoo and D. Kim, eds., *Korean Women in a Struggle for Humanization.* Memphis, TN: The Korean Christian Scholars Publication.

Yu, Eui Young. 1977. "Koreans in America: An Emerging Ethnic Minority." Amerasia Journal 4: 117-131.

_______. 1980a. "Demographic Profile of Koreans in Los Angeles: Size, Composition, and Distribution." A Paper presented at the Koryo Research Institute Workshop, Los Angeles, CA.

_______. 1980b. "Koreans in America: Social and Economic Adjustment." In Byong-Suh Kim, ed., *The Korean Immigrants In America.* New Jersey: The Association of Korean Christian Schools.

_______. 1983. "Korean Communities in America: Past, Present, Future." Amerasia Journal 10: 23-52.

_______. 1990. "Korean American Community in 1989: Issues and Prospects." In H.C. Kim and E. H. Lee, eds., *Koreans in America: Dreams and Realities.* Seoul, Korea: The Institute of Korean Studies.

Yun, Sun Dok. 1975. "Han Guk-Yosong Undong Ui Inyomgwa Banghyang." (The Ideology and Direction of the Korean Women's Movement). *Taehwa (Dialogue).* 8.

APPENDIX:
Questionnaire of Attitudes, Sex Roles, Stress on Wife Abuse

Part I: Demographic Information

1. Age: _____

2. What is your marital status?

(1)	Never married	_____	(4)	Divorced	_____
(2)	Married	_____	(5)	Widowed	_____
(3)	Separated	_____	(6)	Living together	_____

3. What is the highest grade in school you have completed?

(1)	Elementary school (1-6)	_____
(2)	Middle school (7-9)	_____
(3)	High school (9-12)	_____
(4)	2-year college	_____
(5)	4-year college	_____
(6)	Graduate or professional school	_____
(7)	Other (describe)	_____

4. What is your religion?

(1)	Buddhism	_____	(4)	Confucianism	_____
(2)	Protestant	_____	(5)	No religion	_____
(3)	Catholic	_____	(6)	Other (describe)	_____

5. How long have you lived in the United States?

____ years

6. What is your monthly family (you and your husband's) income?

(1) Less than $500_____ (5) 2000-2499 _____
(2) $500-$999 _____ (6) 2500-2999 _____
(3) $1000-$1499 _____ (7) 3000-3999 _____
(4) $1500-$1999 _____ (8) 4000 or more_____

7. Are you employed? Yes _____ No_____

If employed, what is your monthly income? _____

8. Is your husband Korean?

Korean_____ Non-Korean_____

9. With whom do you live now?
(1) Spouse _____
(2) Son(s) _____
(3) Daughter(s) _____
(4) Other relative _____
(5) Friend _____
(6) Grandchildren _____
(7) By myself _____
(8) Other(describe) _____

10. If you live with your children, list ages and sex of children.

____

____

____

11. What is your housing arrangement?

(1) Own home _____
(2) Rented apartment _____
(3) Relative's home _____
(4) Other (describe) _____

Part II: Situational Factors

1. Please answer the following questions: Who does the different chores in your home?

		Wife	Husband	Both
(1)	Cooking	_____	_____	_____
(2)	Washing dishes	_____	_____	_____
(3)	Laundry	_____	_____	_____

(4) Driving the car _____ _____ _____

(5) Shopping for groceries _____ _____ _____

(6) Buying clothes _____ _____ _____

(7) Paying bills _____ _____ _____

(8) Talking to school teacher about children _____ _____ _____

(9) Making bed _____ _____ _____

(10) Cleaning the house _____ _____ _____

(11) Making decisions to buy something _____ _____ _____ (TV, furniture, etc.)

(12) Making decisions to buy a house _____ _____ _____

2. Would you say the relationship between you and your husband is different from when you were in Korea?

_____ Better
_____ Same
_____ Worse

3. May I ask what your job is?

		Now	In Korea
(1)	Unemployed	_____	_____
(2)	Housewife	_____	_____
(3)	Student	_____	_____
(4)	Manual work	_____	_____
(5)	Skilled work	_____	_____
(6)	Clerical, saleswoman	_____	_____
(7)	Semi-professional, manager	_____	_____
(8)	Professional, self-employed	_____	_____

4. May I ask what your husband's job is?

		Now	In Korea
(1)	Unemployed	_____	_____
(2)	Student	_____	_____
(3)	Manual work	_____	_____
(4)	Skilled work	_____	_____

(5)	Clerical, salesman	_____	_____
(6)	Semi-professional, manager	_____	_____
(7)	Professional, self-employed	_____	_____

5. How many times a week do you go out to do work, shopping, or for other things?

(1) Every day _____
(2) 2-3 times a week _____
(3) Once a week _____
(4) 2-3 times a month _____
(5) Hardly ever go out _____

6. What types of friends do you have?

(1) Korean friends _____
(2) American friends _____
(3) Both _____

7. How often do you talk to any of your friends or relatives?

(1) Every day _____
(2) 2-3 times a week _____
(3) Once a week _____
(4) 2-3 times a month _____
(5) Hardly ever _____

8. Do you speak Korean, English, or both languages at home?

   (1) Only Korean ____
   (2) Only English ____
   (3) Both ____

9. How well do you know English?

   (1) Well ____
   (2) A little ____
   (3) Not well ____
   (4) Not at all ____

10. Which newspaper do you read?
    (1) Korean newspaper ____
    (2) American newspaper ____
    (3) Both ____

11. Do you cook only Korean food at home?

    (1) Always ____
    (2) Most of the time ____
    (3) Sometimes ____
    (4) Hardly ever ____

12. Do you drive a car?
    (1) Yes ____
    (2) No ____

13. Do you listen to local news programs on TV or radio?

(1) Always _____
(2) Most of the time _____
(3) Sometimes _____
(4) Hardly ever _____

14. Do you belong to any clubs, churches, or organizations?

(1) Korean churches (temples) _____
(2) Korean association _____
(3) Other social clubs _____
(4) Professional _____
(5) Political groups _____

15. How often do you participate in the activity of those clubs or meetings?

(1) 2-3 times a week _____
(2) Once a week _____
(3) 2-3 times a month _____
(4) Hardly ever _____

Part III: Attitude Toward Korean Traditionalism

1. A Korean woman shouldn't leave her husband once she is already married.

(1) Always _____
(2) Most of the time _____
(3) Sometimes _____
(4) Hardly ever _____

2. Would you say a Korean woman should obey her husband?

(1) Always _____
(2) Most of the time _____
(3) Sometimes _____
(4) Hardly ever _____

3. Do you believe the Korean proverb ("If a hen crows, the household crumbles") ?

(1) Always _____
(2) Most of the time _____
(3) Sometimes _____
(4) Hardly ever _____

4. Do you believe a woman's place is:

(1) To be married, stay home and have children _____
(2) To be married, have children and a career _____
(3) To be married, have no children, and career _____

5. Have you thought about marrying a non-Korean, or only a Korean?

   (1) Korean only ____
   (2) Non-Korean ____
   (3) Both ____

6. Has your marriage been arranged?

   (1) Arranged marriage ____
   (2) Marriage from dating ____
   (3) Combined ____

7. Do you show affection to your husband in public (i.e., holding hands when you walk) ?

   (1) Always ____
   (2) Most of the time ____
   (3) Sometimes ____
   (4) Hardly ever ____

8. Do you say, "I love you" to your husband?

   (1) Always ____
   (2) Most of the time ____
   (3) Sometimes ____
   (4) Hardly ever ____

9. Who makes the most decisions in your home?

(1) Wife _____
(2) Husband _____
(3) Both _____

10. Do you have a joint bank account with your husband, a single account of your own, or both?

(1) Joint _____
(2) Single _____
(3) Both _____

11. Do you cook only Korean food at home?

(1) Always _____
(2) Most of the time _____
(3) Sometimes _____
(4) Hardly ever _____

12. Do you think men are superior to women?

(1) Always _____
(2) Most of the time _____
(3) Sometimes _____
(4) Hardly ever _____

13. Do you prefer a man to be a boss in the home?

(1) Always ______
(2) Most of the time ______
(3) Sometimes ______
(4) Hardly ever ______

14. Suppose you are not married, would you marry a man without your family member's approval?

(1) Yes ______
(2) Perhaps ______
(3) Hardly ever ______
(4) No ______

15. Even if a husband is abusive, a Korean wife should forgive him.

(1) Always ______
(2) Most of the time ______
(3) Sometimes ______
(4) Hardly ever ______

Part IV: The Abuse

1. Please mark any of the items below which apply to you.

(1) My husband/partner yelled at me _____

(2) My husband/partner swore at me _____

(3) My husband/partner destroyed my property _____

(4) My husband/partner threw an object at me _____

(5) My husband/partner threatened to hit me with an object _____

(6) My husband/partner threatened to hit with his fist _____

(7) My husband/partner hit me with a closed fist _____

(8) My husband/partner slapped me _____

(9) My husband/partner hit me with an object _____

(10) My husband/partner threatened me with a knife _____

(11) My husband/partner threatened to kill me _____

(12) My husband/partner threatened to kill himself _____

(13) My husband/partner threatened me with a gun _____

(14) My husband/partner forced me to have sex with him _____

(15) My husband/partner squeezed or pinched me _____

(16) My husband/partner choked me _____

(17) My husband/partner burned me _____

(18) My husband/partner broke one of my bones _____

(19) My husband/partner stabbed me _____

(20) My husband/partner attempted to kill me _____

2. Have you received the following injuries as a result of your husband's abuse?

(1) Bruises _____

(2) Black eye _____

(3) Minor cuts or burns _____

(4) Cuts, burns, or bruises requiring medical attention _____

(5) Concussion _____

(6) Damage to teeth _____

(7) Broken bones _____

(8) Joint injury _____

(9) Spinal injury _____

(10) Injury to internal organs _____

(11) Miscarriage _____

(12) Emotional/mental distress requiring medical care _____

(13) Physical injury requiring hospitalization _____

(14) Other (describe) _____

3. When was the first time your husband was abusive toward you?

(1) In Korea _____
(2) After immigration _____
(3) Not applicable _____

4. On the average, how often have violent or abusive acts taken place?

(1) _________ every day
(2) 1 2 3 4 5 6 (circle one) times a week
(3) 1 2 3 4 (circle one) times a month
(4) 1 2 3 4 5 6 7 8 9 10 11 (circle one) times a year

5. If you have responded to your husband's abuse, place a check in the appropriate column.

(1) Fight back physically _____
(2) Fight back verbally _____
(3) Order him to stop _____
(4) Stare at him _____
(5) Scream for help _____
(6) Cry, beg him to stop _____
(7) Try to protect self _____
(8) Try to leave scene _____
(9) Go stay elsewhere _____
(10) Call police _____
(11) Try to ignore it-do nothing _____

6. What was the opening argument immediately before the incident?

(1) Children _____
(2) Money _____
(3) Sex _____
(4) Religion _____
(5) Outside activity _____
(6) Drinking _____
(7) Watch TV _____

(8)	In-laws & relatives	_____
(9)	Chores and responsibilities	_____
(10)	Food, cooking	_____
(11)	Other men	_____
(12)	Employment	_____
(13)	Friends and associates	_____

7. What do you do after an abusive incident? (Check all responses that occur)

(1)	Cry	_____	(7)	Leave the house	_____
(2)	Apologize	_____	(8)	Go to sleep	_____
(3)	Eat	_____	(9)	Make love	_____
(4)	Drink	_____	(10)	Think about revenge	_____
(5)	Use drugs	_____			
(6)	Watch TV	_____	(11)	Other (describe)	_____

8. Do you know any Korean women which may include yourself who have been battered by their husband?

(1)	Yes	_____
(2)	No	_____
(3)	Don't know	_____

Part V: Stress-Related Symptoms (please check appropriate column)

1. I feel weak all over much of the time.

   (1) Always _____ (3) Sometimes_____
   (2) Most of the time_____ (4) Hardly ever_____

2. I have had periods of days, weeks, or months when I couldn't take care of things because I couldn't "get going."

   (1) Always _____ (3) Sometimes_____
   (2) Most of the time_____ (4) Hardly ever_____

3. In general, would you say that most of the time you are experiencing emotional fluctuations?

   (1) Always _____ (3) Sometimes_____
   (2) Most of the time_____ (4) Hardly ever_____

4. Every so often I suddenly feel hot all over.

   (1) Always _____ (3) Sometimes_____
   (2) Most of the time_____ (4) Hardly ever_____

5. Have you ever been bothered by your heart beating hard?

   (1) Always _____ (3) Sometimes_____
   (2) Most of the time_____ (4) Hardly ever_____

6. Would you say your appetite is changing?

   (1) Always _____ (3) Sometimes_____
   (2) Most of the time_____ (4) Hardly ever_____

7. I have periods of such great restlessness that I cannot sit long in a chain (cannot sit still very long).

   (1) Always _____ (3) Sometimes_____
   (2) Most of the time_____ (4) Hardly ever_____

8. Are you the worrying type (a worrier)?

   (1) Always _____ (3) Sometimes_____
   (2) Most of the time_____ (4) Hardly ever_____

9. Have you ever been bothered by shortness of breath when you were not exercising or working hard?

   (1) Always _____ (3) Sometimes_____
   (2) Most of the time_____ (4) Hardly ever_____

10. Are you ever bothered by nervousness (irritable, fidgety, tense)?

(1) Always _____ (3) Sometimes_____
(2) Most of the time_____ (4) Hardly ever_____

11. Have you ever had any fainting spells (lost consciousness)?

(1) Always _____ (3) Sometimes_____
(2) Most of the time_____ (4) Hardly ever_____

12. Do you ever have any trouble in getting to sleep or staying asleep?

(1) Always _____ (3) Sometimes_____
(2) Most of the time_____ (4) Hardly ever_____

13. I am bothered by acid (sour) stomach several times a week.

(1) Always _____ (3) Sometimes_____
(2) Most of the time_____ (4) Hardly ever_____

14. My memory seems to be all right (good).

(1) Always _____ (3) Sometimes_____
(2) Most of the time_____ (4) Hardly ever_____

15. Have you ever been bothered by "cold sweats"?

(1) Always _____ (3) Sometimes_____
(2) Most of the time_____ (4) Hardly ever_____

16. Do your hands ever tremble enough to bother you?

(1) Always _____ (3) Sometimes_____
(2) Most of the time_____ (4) Hardly ever_____

17. There seems to be a fullness (congestion) in my head or nose much of the time.

(1) Always _____ (3) Sometimes_____
(2) Most of the time_____ (4) Hardly ever_____

18. I have personal worries that get me down physically (make me physically ill) .

(1) Always _____ (3) Sometimes_____
(2) Most of the time_____ (4) Hardly ever_____

19. Do you feel somewhat apart even among friends (apart, isolated, alone)?

(1) Always _____ (3) Sometimes_____
(2) Most of the time_____ (4) Hardly ever_____

20. Nothing ever turns out for me the way I want it to (turns out, happens, comes about, i.e., my wishes aren't fulfilled).

(1) Always _____ (3) Sometimes_____
(2) Most of the time_____ (4) Hardly ever_____

21. Are you ever troubled with headaches or pains in the head?

(1) Always _____ (3) Sometimes_____
(2) Most of the time_____ (4) Hardly ever_____

22. You sometimes can't help wondering if anything is worthwhile anymore.

(1) Always _____ (3) Sometimes_____
(2) Most of the time_____ (4) Hardly ever_____

23. Have you had a thought about suicide?

(1) Always _____ (3) Sometimes_____
(2) Most of the time_____ (4) Hardly ever_____

24. Have you attempted suicide?
(1) Always _____ (3) Sometimes_____
(2) Most of the time_____ (4) Hardly ever_____

Part VI: Service Utilization

1. If you have a personal problem, how would you solve it?

(1) Time will solve ______
(2) Keep it in the family ______
(3) Consulting friends, relatives ______
(4) Professional counseling ______
(5) Other (describe) ______

2. When you are in a crisis, where would you go for help?

(1) Husband ______
(2) Relatives ______
(3) Friends, neighbors ______
(4) Minister ______
(5) Private clinic ______
(6) Social service agency ______
(7) Other (describe) ______
(8) No place ______

3a. If you know of any formal sources of help, how did you learn about them?

(1) Through friends ______
(2) Through Korean community center ______
(3) Through Korean church ______
(4) Through Korean newspaper ______
(5) Through social service agency ______
(6) Other (describe) ______

3b. If you don't, what are the reasons for lack of your knowledge?

(1) Language barrier _____
(2) Never interested _____
(3) Don't know where to go _____
(4) Other (describe) _____

4. Have you ever seen a professional person or been to professional place for help?

(1) Yes _____
(2) No _____

5. If you know of formal sources of help and need to seek help, yet don't utilize those sources, what stops you from using those services?

(1) Transportation problem _____
(2) Language barrier _____
(3) Shameful to friends and neighbors _____
(4) Family rejection _____
(5) Don't know how to approach _____
(6) Other (describe) _____

6. What would you consider as most needed services for the Korean battered woman?

____
____
____

7. In what types of programs do you mostly want to participate?

____
____
____

SUBJECT INDEX